TEN COMMANDMENTS

for Pastors Leaving a Congregation

TEN COMMANDMENTS

for Pastors Leaving a Congregation

Lawrence W. Farris

William B. Eerdmans Publishing Company

Grand Rapids, Michigan / Cambridge, U.K.

Wm. B. Eerdmans Publishing Co.
255 Jefferson Ave. S.E., Grand Rapids, Michigan 49503 /
P.O. Box 163, Cambridge CB3 9PU U.K.

Printed in the United States of America

11 10 09 08 07 06   7 6 5 4 3 2 1

Library of Congress Cataloging-in-Publication Data

Farris, Lawrence W.
Ten commandments for pastors leaving a congregation /
Lawrence W. Farris
p.   cm.
ISBN-10: 0-8028-2924-4
ISBN-13: 978-0-8028-2924-5 (pbk.: alk. paper)
1. Clergy — Relocation.   2. Clergy — Appointment,
call, and election.   I. Title.

BV664.F37   2006
253′.2 — dc22

2006014254

www.eerdmans.com

In Gratitude to

Fred Cunningham
Matthew Deames
Steve Doughty
Helen Havlik
Richard Jackson
Linda Knieriemen
Jonathan Knight
Nelson Lumm
Philip Lyon
Amy Gall Ritchie
Marilyn Schlimgen
Cindy Skutar
Bobby Joe Tolbert
Alice Fleming Townley
Seth Weeldreyer

Pastors creative and faithful
with whom I have been privileged to journey

114395

Contents

Acknowledgments

The congregations I have served have each been remarkably gracious when I concluded my ministries with them. In each case, the congregations of the First Presbyterian Church of Annapolis, Maryland, the Okemos Presbyterian Church of Okemos, Michigan, and the First Presbyterian Church of Three Rivers-Centreville, Michigan, sent me forth with gratitude, acceptance, and a sense of empowerment for the ministry that lay ahead. They blessed me with a clear sense of what we had accomplished together that helped me know how I had grown as a pastor and believer while I was with them. I am deeply grateful to the people of those congregations for these gifts.

I am also grateful to those pastors, from a variety of denominations, who have shared the dimensions of their own good departings with me — as well as to those who shared accounts of trials and tribulations when the parting was painful. Their stories, along with those from clergy I have been privileged to counsel and accompany personally as they made a pastoral transition, have been invaluable to me. These women and men have broadened my understanding of the dynamics of leave-taking and have allowed the distillation which follows to come clear.

I have changed the names of all these pastors in the following pages, but their faces, whether glowing with satisfaction or wrenched with tearful hurt, remain clear in my mind and heart.

As always, my love and far-beyond-words gratitude go to my beloved family — my patient and encouraging wife Pat, my enthusiastic and day-brightening son Jordan, my wise and insightful daughter Rachel — for their graceful incarnating of God's love again and again and again. In them, the face of God is ever revealed. Their constancy in reminding me how all things intermingle for good for those who love God is a gift beyond price or measure.

Introduction

Good endings to pastorates open the door, for both pastor and congregation, to promising futures of new faithfulness to God's work in the world. Abbreviated, curt, lack-of-closure endings, on the other hand, encumber both pastor and congregation with unnecessary burdens that will impair new beginnings. In the best of circumstances, leaving a pastorate can be an occasion for celebration and gratitude. The ministry created and brought to fruition through the pastor's relationship with a congregation can be celebrated as God is praised for what has been accomplished during the pastor's tenure. The pastor can be thanked for the leadership he has offered; the congregation can be thanked for the responsiveness they have shown. Both pastor and people can rejoice in growth in faith; both can laugh at lessons learned through folly; both can weep for sorrows shared. Even at the close of a good pastorate, however, there are other feelings to be acknowledged. And there is work to be done in order for both pastor and congregation to be free to embrace the future gladly and expectantly.

Sometimes leaving a pastorate, especially a good and faithful one, can feel like nothing so much as a death. A pastor has for some number of years been pouring energy into a relationship with a congregation, and now that relationship is ending. The relationship has been rich and complex, marked as any relationship will be by strengths and weaknesses, to be sure, with the balance hopefully towards the former. Now in the congregation there is sadness, perhaps anger, maybe a sense of rejection, certainly a measure of grief. The departing pastor often shares some of the sadness and sense of loss even as these feelings are mingled with expectation of what lies ahead. One temptation on the pastor's part is to mask the pain of this loss with excitement about a new position and its possibilities, or the anticipated pleasures of retirement; another is to flee as quickly as possible and to let others clean up whatever mess of hurt is left behind. But pastors who have sat with the dying and their families know that such illusory denials do not work. And they are not what God intends when partings come.

In other situations, when the pastor-congregation relationship has been painful and strife-ridden, leaving can feel like a divorce. There can be anger, blame, and mutual recrimination for a history of hurts inflicted by both parties. There can be feelings of relief now that the party deemed responsible for the pain will no longer be present. But there is also the possibility for forgiveness and learning as the relationship ends. Again, the pastor's temptation to flee to a situation which is assumed to be better merely for being different is fraught with danger, as is the congregation's certainty that all will be well once the so-and-so is off the premises. Both need to remember that we are called in our faith to work toward reconciliation.

It is not as rare as one might think, or hope, that congregations sometimes call similar pastors (sometimes even in physical appearance!) time after time. And no one should be surprised that the same congregational problems keep arising pastor after pastor in such circumstances. Likewise, some pastors keep finding themselves in congregations with similar types of problems. And they should not be surprised at the commonality they keep seeking out at some preconscious level. When scripture says that the sins of the fathers and mothers are visited upon successive generations (Exodus 20:5), it's not just because God is jealous. It's because people often choose not to learn from their mistakes and thereby keep repeating the same patterns of brokenness. What's the popular definition of insanity? Doing the same thing over and over again and expecting different results. Without seeking good partings, both pastors and congregations can be prone to repeating previous mistakes.

How a pastor leaves a congregation is crucial for the pastor's future work and well-being as well for the congregation's. The time of parting affords an often-missed opportunity for learning and clarification, for healing and forgiveness. It is a time when persistent negative patterns can be identified and altered; it is a time when cherished traditions can be honored and sustained. If the leave-taking is done with honesty and intentionality and as much compassion as possible, the aforementioned gifts can bring new life to both parties. And it is to that end that these ten commandments are offered.

As I said in my previous book, *Ten Commandments for Pastors New to a Congregation,* these commandments differ in a crucial way from their biblical counterparts. Clarence Jordan, founder of the Koinonia Farms Community in Georgia, once observed that the biblical Ten Commandments are like natural laws, such as the law of gravity, in that we cannot break them. When we do violate them, it is we who are broken, and in those instances we serve only as illustrations of the commandments' wisdom and truth. These commandments for departing pastors are not like natural law. They can, and most likely will, be broken by every departing pastor, to a greater or lesser extent. Blessedly, we are forgiven our mistakes, both by God and usually by the congregations with whom we have been in ministry, in order that we might learn from them.

Finally, the rule, "Don't let the urgent crowd out the important!" applies to the departing pastor as surely as it does to the new pastor. I believe the ten commandments I have set forth in this book are important, even if they do not bear the weight of natural law. And it is my hope that pastors who attend to them will have an easier and more faithful ending to their ministries, an ending that sets them free for whatever future is before them. Avoiding some of the more common pitfalls of a departing will, I pray, bring blessing to both pastor and congregation that both may continue to glorify God and nourish Christ's church in faithfulness to its calling.

· I ·

Thou Shalt Know
When It Is Time to Go

*"For everything there is a season, and a time for
every purpose under heaven."*

ECCLESIASTES 3:1

There are many reasons for leaving a pastorate: retirement, a call to a new ministry, congregational conflict in
which the pastor plays a significant part. Each of these situations has unique aspects, but all require pastors to look
with profound honesty at their ministry and when it is
time for it to conclude. The pastor in any of these situations must honestly discern and balance what is best for
him or her as well as what is best for the congregation.
This is a task best undertaken with those who know both
the congregation and the pastor well. Family, close
friends, colleagues, and denominational representatives
may all be part of the discernment process, provided they
understand its confidential nature. Few actions can undermine a ministry more quickly than the leaked-out word
that the pastor is contemplating leaving. Depending on
the situation, the congregational response can be one of

anger, sorrow, anxiety, or even eager anticipation, all of which will often negatively impact its ministry by diverting energy away from service to questions of leadership.

How does a pastor know when it is time to leave? Long, comfortable, satisfying pastorates may keep that question on the back burner — so much so that it might not even be on the stove. By contrast, highly conflicted pastorates in which the pastor is enmeshed in the conflict may relentlessly push the question into everyone's consciousness. But as most pastors will move at least a few times over the course of their ministry, and all will one day retire, the question is inevitable. Giving some regular attention to it — perhaps on a yearly basis during a retreat time or in consultation with a spiritual director or mentor or supervisor — is the first step in leaving well. Asking, "When do I leave?" is a crucial and ongoing aspect of evaluating the impact and continuing value of pastoral leadership.

Even at the beginning of a new pastorate, pastors can consider the question of how long to stay — not in the sense of looking ahead to their own next call, but in the sense of looking back over the congregation's history to gain some idea of what the average length of stay has been for previous pastors. Sometimes congregations will show remarkable consistency in having pastors who stay about eight to ten years and then move on. In churches prone to conflict, the turnover time may be considerably shorter. Awareness of such patterns can help new pastors sense when conflict may arise or congregational restlessness may emerge.

Long pastorates can be very valuable in establishing congregational stability. But they can also create two significant congregational problems: the first is that of comfortable lethargy, and the second, much more problematic in the long run, is that of an inability to accept any style of pastoral leadership save that modeled by the long-serving and beloved pastor. The latter can lead to a succession of short pastorates after the sainted pastor leaves as the congregation grinds up one pastor after another in its quest to replicate the single style of ministry that has been deemed acceptable and worthy.

On the other hand, pastors who move of their own volition with regularity after fairly short pastorates (fewer than four years is usually considered short) may need to ask themselves if they are simply repeating the same patterns, sermonic and programmatic, over and over with different congregations rather than entering into the sustained relationships, greater theological maturity, and deeper congregational ministries that are usually possible over the course of a longer pastorate. Moving too quickly too regularly can be a sign that the pastor's own growth is somewhat stunted. The impact of such pastors on the churches they serve, while sometimes dramatic, does not often enhance long-term congregational faithfulness to Christ's call to service.

Retirement

In most cases, retirement is the easiest leave-taking to do well, since the date for leaving is generally dictated by age. But the question still arises: how much advance notice should the pastor give the congregation prior to departure? The short answer is that enough time should be given to allow the congregation to express their appreciation and the pastor to say his goodbyes, but not so much that the congregation begins to wonder if the day of retirement will ever arrive. A guideline of about three months' notice works well in most pastorates.

The succeeding chapters will explore how this period is to be used, but special circumstances may warrant extending this three-month period. If the pastor is concluding a long pastorate of fifteen years or more, or if the pastor has been the only pastor the congregation has ever known (as sometimes happens in new church development work where the organizing pastor continues on in an extended period of service), then a longer period of leave-taking is warranted. This time can be used by a respected and beloved leader to prepare her congregation to receive another — and another style of — leader.

Pastor Paul had served his church for twenty-seven years, years marked by growth in numbers of parishioners and ministries. His congregation had granted him three sabbaticals during his tenure, and he had wisely used these to refresh his spirit and to explore new ways of being in ministry. But he was worried that his impending retirement would be traumatic for the congregation, as many church members had virtually no other experience with any style of ministry except his. Furthermore, he had seen a neighboring church go through enormous turmoil after a long-serving and very capable pastor retired. That congregation could not find a clone of their retired pastor and seemed incapable of accepting any other style of leadership. Paul had the opportunity to examine the materials the neighboring church was using as it searched for a new minister (its third since the sainted pastor's retirement), and he was astonished to see among them a letter from the retiree which said, in essence, that the only path to success was to imitate him in work, devotion, love, and service!

Out of love for the congregation he had felt privileged to have lived with for so many years, Paul announced his retirement a full year ahead of time. Furthermore, he submitted to his governing board a detailed assessment of his strengths and weaknesses as a pastor as well as those of the congregation. He also asked the board to initiate a process of exploring various styles of ministry with the congregation, a process of which he would not be a part. Finally, he asked his board and denominational officials to begin the process of securing a competent interim pastor to follow him, preferably one who was distinctly different from him in age, gender, and previous place of service.

The board was reluctant at first to accept this task, partly out of affection and partly out of grief over Paul's impending retirement. But they initiated a series of congregational discussions moderated by other clergy from their denomination in which Paul's assessment was reviewed. As these conversations unfolded, much satisfaction with Paul's leadership was shared and celebrated, but dreams for the congregation's future also began to emerge. The clergy moderating the discussions were themselves different from Paul, and simply by their presence they began to model alternative styles. The information shared at these conversations was recorded and synthesized by the board for use as it sought new pastoral leadership. The clergy moderators were invited to share their observations with the board and also to preach when Paul was away during his concluding year. Again, this provided some initial, and conscious, exposure to ministerial styles different from Paul's. And after Paul's departure, a skilled interim pastor who was a woman was appointed to lead the congregation for at least a year to allow sufficient time for the congregation to live with different leadership while beginning the search for a successor to, rather than a replacement of, Paul. After almost two years, a new pastor was called. She was twenty years Paul's junior, had grown up in a different part of the country, had attended a different seminary, and had a significantly different style in the pulpit, in committee work, and in her programmatic emphases. And she succeeded well.

The problem sometimes arises, more frequently than one might suspect in a vocation whose practitioners are prone to burnout, that a pastor seems unable to retire. Members of the congregation are aware that retirement age has been attained, but no word is heard of whether or not the pastor is leaving. If the church is stagnating (more on that below) under the retirement-eligible pastor's continuing leadership, this can be particularly problematic. The situation is most likely to occur when a pastor has failed to develop interests outside his vocation. In other words, the pastor may not only not know what to do if he retires, but more deeply, who he is if he's not in ministry. There can be a crisis of identity, even at this age, and it sometimes leads to pastors working on and on (or, as some others do, taking interim pastorate after interim pastorate) well past the point of effectiveness.

Furthermore, it may be difficult for the governing board or congregation to broach the subject of retirement with such a pastor because of reluctance to be seen as forcing the pastor out. Pastors need to have interests beyond the walls of the church and functions of ministry, and these need to be developed in advance of retirement. The adage is true that a successful retirement happens when one has something to retire to.

The Reverend Martha loved being a pastor. Single and a second-career minister, her work brought satisfaction, even joy, to her. Martha loved everything about ministry — preaching and leading worship, pastoral care, teaching, going on mission trips. At age sixty-eight, she knew she was slowing down, but her work still afforded more than satisfaction: it was who she felt herself to be. Members of her board appreciated her and in no way wished to hurt her feelings, but they also understandably wondered when she would retire since Martha had not said a word about it. Eventually, Martha's wise denominational executive raised the matter of retirement with Martha. After some initial sadness and sobering reflection on how she had denied the reality of her age, Martha asked if she might go to part-time ministry at another church. Her executive said there might very well be places where Martha's gifts and experience could be used well, but she also set the condition that Martha was to work with her on creating a dream for her eventual retirement. Martha did this after moving to an interim position, and by the time she was seventy years old, she was ready to move on to a life of grandmothering, travel, writing, and volunteering that she continues to enjoy.

The flip side of Martha's retirement-postponing love of ministry is the pastor who has had it with ministry and who is just hanging on until the day, long marked on the calendar, when he or she will be eligible for retirement. Such pastors are often burned out or bored (more on that below) and need to seek the counsel of denominational officers for help in finding another form of service to take them to retirement. The inertia that besets a congregation that has been waiting for its pastor to retire can be substantial, and a substantial problem for the next pastor.

Jack was such a pastor. Tired of preaching, of pastoral calling, of listening to complaints, of going to meetings, he was at the point of wondering how he would ever last the remaining two years until the blessed day when he could leave it all to someone else. He was free enough from denial to know his congregation knew he was ready to be done, and he felt guilty for just marking time. After a couple of months of feeling stuck in this situation, Jack contacted his bishop to ask for help. The bishop was most understanding and found Jack a part-time administrative position at a denominational retreat and conference center. This allowed Jack to complete with dignity what had been a good life in ministry with several churches. And it allowed his church to find the leadership they deserved.

Call to a New Ministry

Most pastors will serve several churches over the course of their ministry. Moving from one field of service to another alters life significantly and is not something to be undertaken lightly. How does one know when it's time for a change of venue? The wise pastor will listen for the various promptings of the Spirit and trust the Spirit to lead.

A common way in which a pastor comes to awareness of the need for a change is through a sense of satisfaction and completion in the present work. As one pastor put it, it's time to think about leaving when one has moved the congregation to greater faithfulness through the right use of one's gifts, and any further growth can only be accomplished through a massive retooling. It is, of course, tempting to remain and savor the fruits of one's labor, but too much of that can lead a pastor to coast right into stagnation, both for herself and for the congregation she is serving. Regular sabbaticals or the wise use of continuing education leave can provide new possibilities for the pastor, but there comes a time when what can be done has been done. Often the time to consider departing comes when a major project — a building renovation, a new mission commitment — has been completed.

If this sense of satisfaction and completion is ignored, a pastor may very well begin to feel stagnant or restless. When events like new member classes, youth retreats, stewardship campaigns, and officer training workshops evoke a sense of foreboding or even dread at the thought of "the same old, same old," the Spirit may be nudging the pastor towards a new context with new challenges and possibilities. When a pastor feels like he or she has "heard it all before" in calling on members, or begins to notice thoughts like, "I wonder what it's like elsewhere," or "Is this all there is?" it's time to start thinking about a move.

Pastor Janet was coasting along in the ninth year of her second pastorate. Life within and without the congregation was good — worship attendance was high and steady; membership had increased slowly but steadily over the years; her standing in the community was good; denominational work, especially with candidates for ministry, brought her significant satisfaction. A project to remodel the church offices had been completed and paid off early, much to the delight and improved morale of her staff. But several times in conversation with other pastors, Janet heard herself saying, "Yup, I'm about to start my fourth time through the lectionary." She loved preaching and wondered why this comment had started haunting her since all the outward signs of her work were so positive. She brought the remark up with her spiritual director and initiated a time of prayerful discernment. Several months later she began to seek a new call. Her comment? "I decided to leave while the party was going strong." After her departure, which was marked by a great outpouring of gratitude, the congregation continued its strong functioning, and Janet found herself in a redeveloping congregation that led her down several new and rewarding paths she was delighted to explore.

Beyond satisfaction and stagnation lies boredom. The Spirit will get our attention somehow! And if the pastor is bored, he is very likely to become boring to the very people he's supposed to be leading. If the pastor is bored, the people will likely be, too. The impact of boredom on any church's ministry will be negative and significant, greatly increasing the struggle of a new pastor to create momentum in the congregation's life. Waiting until boredom sets in makes the work of moving more difficult since boredom, like its cousin depression, is an enervating emotion.

But a new call can emerge from without as well as from within. Out of the blue, a pastor receives a call from a colleague to ask whether he might be interested in such and such a church. Or a denominational leader drops by to inquire whether he has ever thought about leaving parish work for administrative leadership. Or his eye falls on an advertisement in a journal in which a church is seeking a pastor and the description of the position sounds like it was written precisely for him. Sometimes, perhaps especially when congregational life is flowing along well and no thought of a move has arisen, an opportunity may present itself unexpectedly. How does scripture put it? "Behold, I am doing a new thing" (Isaiah 43:19; Revelation 21:5). A willingness to be surprised can open the way to a new field of service.

Whether the Spirit works through inner experience or outward possibility, a discerning pastor will listen deeply and prayerfully, and seek the counsel of trusted companions and mentors to see if the time has come to make a change.

Congregational Conflict

All congregations have conflicts, some small-scale, some large-scale. And for this reason, conflict management has become an increasingly significant part of many pastors' training in recent years. Congregations become healthier when conflict is openly faced rather than repressed; repression only serves to increase the potential for explosive damage at a later date.

But it sometimes happens that the pastor cannot mediate congregational conflict because he or she is the focus of the conflict. Other problems arise when the pastor has become identified with one side or another of the contending congregational parties. When either situation occurs, intervention by an outside mediator is warranted, and it may well be that the pastor will need to leave for healing to occur.

The Reverend Rod experienced a conversion to pacifism while on a peacemaking trip sponsored by his denomination to a third-world country. Prior to this experience, he had been liberal in his politics, but had espoused the just war theory as an acceptable Christian position. Upon his return from the trip, Rod began an extended study of Christian pacifism and invited those of the congregation who were interested to join him. Some did and found the study compelling. Rod began preaching regularly on pacifism, to the point that it began to seem to some members that he preached on nothing else. A group in his congregation met with him and, with considerable graciousness, affirmed both his right to preach as he felt led and his commitment to pacifism. But they asked for more balance in his preaching, that he touch on other issues that were part of the Christian experience. Rod responded with an intense insistence that he would preach on what he believed was the most urgent issue before the Christian church, and that issue was pacifism. However much at odds Rod was feeling with the congregation, he chose to ignore those feelings. And the consequences were painful.

Attendance started to drop drastically thereafter, and denominational mediators were brought in to work with Rod and the congregation. It came out that Rod was seen not only as being too narrowly focused, but also as neglecting pastorally those members who disagreed with him. But Rod was unyielding in his commitment. While affirming his right to preach as he believed himself called, the denominational officials also faulted him for his neglect of other issues and some members. Rod was given a six-month period in which to bring balance back to his ministry. No changes ensued, and he was then given six months to find another church or other employment. Rod finally left without having secured any new position. The church survived, but lost quite a few members who believed not only that Rod had been wrong, but also that the denomination had not acted swiftly or decisively enough in addressing the situation he had created. Some years and two pastors later, the congregation has recovered its strength both in numbers and in ministry, but the road to recovery was long and difficult.

Similar problems may arise when a pastor sides with one group against another in the midst of congregational conflict, and thereby moves out of a moderating role. Sometimes this is inevitable, particularly in congregations where a small minority has a long history of antagonism toward pastors or the general direction in which the church is moving. A pastor may weather such conflict, although often at considerable personal cost, if she is willing to extend pastoral care to the dissenters while being clear where her convictions lie. Here again, assistance from denominational officials may be invaluable, both to the pastor personally and to the congregation.

The Reverend Mary was welcomed by the majority of her congregation, who valued her skilled leading of worship and faithful pastoral care. But a group of four families constantly criticized aspects of the church generally, and Mary particularly. The main point of contention was the youth program. The critics felt Mary wasn't doing enough to teach morals to the youth and that the youth group spent too much time on fellowship activities and service projects, and not enough on moral education. The criticism wore on Mary as she encountered it regularly. It began to seem to her that someone, and not just the critics, was always asking, "What's going on with the youth program?"

The Christian education committee had, with Mary's assistance, found good materials for parents to use with their youth at home and had developed classes and small groups centered on Christian parenting. The naysayers refused to attend these and continued to contend that Mary wasn't doing her job. So Mary asked several colleagues to form a group to assess the church's education ministry and to hear the complainers out. These pastors found the congregation's youth ministry far above average — and they were immediately denounced by the same four families as biased in Mary's favor. Mary began to feel that the best, and certainly the easiest, action she could take would be to leave.

But she liked the congregation and felt good about her work, so Mary decided to stick it out. She made clear her support of the education committee whenever she was asked, and also made sure to include the dissenting families in her pastoral care just as she would any other church members. Three of the families eventually left for other churches, while the one with the longest-standing ties to the congregation remained. The controversy died down to an occasional snide remark, the youth program flourished, and Mary stayed for several more years. She did confide to her colleagues that had the contentious members not left or if the unhappy portion of the congregation had grown significantly, she would have chosen to leave rather than to further contribute to the division. Most felt this would have been as wise a decision as the one to stay under the prevailing circumstances.

DISCERNMENT IS an essential work of ministry in many areas, but perhaps no place more so than in the matter of when to move. Discernment must always have an inward and an outward dimension. The inward aspect seeks to sense how the Spirit is leading us as it whispers in our hearts. Here we are attentive to what we are feeling and to what we hear ourselves saying. In the outward dimension, we assess what is afoot in the congregation and attend to what others are saying to us that might point us toward change. Regular and honest attention to both sides of the question, "Is it time?" will guide pastors to good decisions. And such attention will ultimately bless both the pastor and the congregation.

Thou Shalt Explain Thyself

"About this we have much to say which is hard to explain."

HEBREWS 5:11A

Whatever the reason for making a pastoral move, once the decision has been made, it is essential to explain it to the congregation to the best of one's ability. For pastors in episcopally-governed denominations, it will not suffice merely to blame the move on the powers that be. For pastors not in such denominations, neither will it suffice to attribute the decision utterly and entirely to the immutable call of God, as if one had no say in the matter whatsoever. Congregations have a right to know what is moving in the departing pastor's heart. And they can be deepened in their own journey by the pastor's considered explanation of what is afoot in his or her faith journey that has led to the decision to move to a new call.

Retirement is generally the easiest pastoral transition to explain, since it is expected at a certain age. Nevertheless, the retiring pastor will do well to articulate what his or her ministry has meant, not just with the final congregation, but in total (many members will not have a clear picture of the various stops along the pastor's vocational journey). Not only will such a retrospective give the pastor the opportunity to attend to the matter of what his or her vocational life has meant, it also will set before the congregation what a lifetime of faithfulness looks like. Many people are drawn to the faith and the church because they perceive a need for meaning in their lives. They know the goals of secular culture, even if well achieved, will not confer the sense of value they long for, come the end of life's journey. The retiring pastor's reflections on how ministry has created meaning can be a moment of particular encouragement. It is often so easy (and understandable) for the church to get excessively focused on the details of being the community of faith — after all, church school teachers must be found, stewardship campaigns devised and run, and all the rest. A pastor's retirement speech or sermon offers the opportunity to describe specifically what a life devoted to God's service and glory has looked like. As an explanation, this parting gift can be nothing less than inspirational to those seeking this in their own lives.

The situation is different for the pastor moving to another congregation, particularly if church life is going well. In many denominations, congregants understand that it is the pastor who initiates the quest for a new call. But even if the pastor did not initiate the move, people want to know how he or she feels about it. They want to know why. And they have a right to know. Glib, evasive, "It isn't up to me" answers will not do.

What will do is the thoughtful sharing of what deliberations the pastor has gone through in contemplating this change. The occasion of a move gives the pastor an excellent opportunity to speak theologically about what is meant by the term "call" in the particular tradition of which the congregation is a part. What is the combination of internal and external considerations that help Christians discern a call? What are the roles of prayer, spiritual guidance, consultation with others? Making a vocational change is not, after all, an experience restricted to the clergy. All Christians, to a greater or lesser extent depending on their tradition, have some understanding of being called to serve God. All Christians want to live in a way pleasing to God and not just to themselves. How does a layperson comprehend the concept of calling? As the departing pastor explains the inward and outward movement in her life, she can help the members of her congregation begin to comprehend how they, too, might better sense the leading of God.

Often the call to a new church needs to be explained primarily in terms of its timing (naming the sense of a chapter being completed in the congregation's life) or in terms of the draw of new challenges (being specific about how the new call will push the pastor to grow as a servant of God). Congregations understand that even the most beloved pastors are not going to stay forever; what they need is an adequate explanation of, "Why now?" and, "What is leading you onward?" The specific naming of what has been accomplished with the congregation and of what possibilities lie ahead for the pastor will ease most minds and make the transition at least understandable, if not palatable. Such explanations can be made in various ways: orally, in sermons or at a farewell dinner; or in writing, in congregational letters or newsletter articles; or in a combination of these (more on this in Chapter Four).

Pastor John was known by his congregation to be faithful in his devotional life. Some thought of him as a bit of a mystic, and many were aware that he met regularly with a spiritual director, although some were not entirely sure what this discipline involved. When John was called to a new position as associate pastor for spiritual life in a large congregation after his twelve-year pastorate, he embraced this change as an opportunity to share, and thereby gently nudge his congregation toward, the intentional work of discernment.

John gave a series of sermons over his last two months expressly intended to clarify what spiritual disciplines are, what they meant in his life, and how he had come to clarity that he should seek a new call. He invited his spiritual director to one Sunday service and had her lead part of the liturgy. He talked about his disciplines as a way of constantly asking what God would have him do and be, both in day-to-day life and in the larger arc of his spiritual journey with and to God. Many of his congregants worked in professions in which they were often confronted with the possibility of, and sometimes the requirement to, relocate. Because these were difficult matters to confront, John's sermons were widely welcomed as offering a spiritual perspective on the tension between Christian vocation and secular employment. In other words, John's openness about his process opened up new resources for members to consider their own vocational transitions as part of their spiritual life. John left feeling not only that he was better known and understood by his congregation, but also that his parting teaching had been empowering to it.

Other pastoral transitions are more difficult to explain. If the congregation has experienced severe or sustained conflict, and particularly if the pastor has been directly involved in the conflict, an explanation of the move may be dicey. Those opposed to him may be nothing so much as relieved that the troubling pastor is leaving, and not be terribly interested in explanations regarding his reasons. On the other hand, those sympathetic to the pastor may understand that he is tired of the fight, but still feel abandoned and need some word of assurance. Still others not directly involved in the conflict may feel the pastor is bailing out of a difficult situation, a choice that may be perceived as either weak or unprofessional. Can the departing pastor respond to all of these feelings and agendas equally effectively? Probably not, but an effort still needs to be made.

Pastor Becky was part of the problem, and she knew it. She had led her congregation into developing a contemporary style of worship that had proven popular in many quarters and had led to a significant increase in congregational membership. While making this change, she had continued to lead a more traditional second service, which was smaller in attendance and appreciated primarily by older members. But it was clear to everyone that her heart was in the contemporary service, especially since she played keyboard and sang in the praise band.

Becky found it hard to maintain the same energy for worship in the two contrasting services. She often hinted, not too subtly, that those attending the traditional service should expose themselves to the new service, or that efforts should be made to find a blended style. The traditionalists shot back that they were the bearers of the denomination's long traditions in liturgy and music, and they did not want to see these die out in the church they had so long served and supported. Rather than switch to new worship forms, the old-timers thought Becky should make a greater effort to teach the meaning and value of denominational traditions to new members and young people.

The two services continued in parallel, and gradually the congregation divided along the lines of who attended which service. As dissatisfaction among the traditionalists grew, total financial receipts started to decline. It was clear that the contemporary service contingent did not give as faithfully or as generously as the traditionalists. The board began to struggle with where to make cuts in staff and program. Becky became more and more enmeshed in the conflict and more and more burdened by it. Finally, in consulting with denominational officials, Becky decided to seek a call to a church committed to contemporary worship. And, in part because of her fine musicianship, she was successful.

With considerable grace, Becky explained, even confessed, at a surprisingly well attended farewell dinner, her own role in the conflict, and she made clear that the point had long since passed at which she could effectively manage its resolution. She shared that she would be pursuing continuing education in conflict management in the future, having learned that this was a significant area of pastoral weakness for her. Without becoming defensive, Becky affirmed how much her pastoral work with all members, even those with whom she had been in conflict, had meant to her. She explained that she had asked the denomination to bring in a conflict mediation team to help the congregation resolve its struggles as it moved toward calling a new pastor. While congregational feelings about Becky remained divided, many on both sides of the conflict felt that she had shown a good measure of wisdom in the choices she made in her leaving.

Another transition in which a measure of confession is in order is in the case in which there is simply a mismatch between pastor and congregation. A common sign of such a mismatch is a dramatically shortened "honeymoon" period, which in typical pastorates lasts from twelve to eighteen months, and a rapidly emerging sense of restlessness in either or both parties. If it becomes clear within the first few months that this pastor and this congregation do not belong together or cannot do ministry together by virtue of theological differences, personality problems, or an unwillingness to change, a dissolution of the pastoral relationship may be in order. Such a mismatch is usually the result of self-deception on the part of the pastor, the congregation, or both. Yet if the pastor in such cases is willing to submit to focused mentoring and further training to make needed changes in his or her approach to ministry, the situation may be salvaged. If not, a move should probably be contemplated to avoid further damage to both pastor and congregation.

But whether the pastor leaves of his own volition or is asked to leave, it is crucial that both he and the congregation engage in supervised self-examination to learn why such a mismatch occurred. Did the congregation, when seeking a new pastor, misrepresent itself in terms of its identity, its traditions, its dreams, and what it wanted in a pastor? Or did the pastor overstate his qualifications or experience, or conceal some deeply held beliefs clearly at odds with those of the congregation? If there has been clear deception by one party or the other, the temptation to blame will be strong indeed.

II

In the mismatch situation, after honest self-examination is done with the help of professionals, the departing pastor may be able to name what she has learned and perhaps call the congregation to greater clarity about itself as well. But to avoid further damage, it is crucial that she share this honest assessment without succumbing to the temptation to blame the congregation lest the opportunity for at least some growth and learning be lost.

Pastor Joe had effectively served two smaller churches before being called to a large, urban church where his predecessor had been an accomplished preacher and administrator. Joe himself was a skilled preacher, and it was having that gift affirmed which led him to accept this new, and quite different, call. But within weeks, Joe realized he missed the intimacy of the smaller churches. He hadn't realized how much he enjoyed pastoral work, work that in his new church was handled by other staff and lay ministers. Furthermore, he found his creativity waning under the pressure to administer a large and complex church organization. What had seemed like a big step up the professional ladder now seemed like a mistake that was going to leave him feeling isolated and unhappy.

For the church's part, the board affirmed Joe's preaching skills but realized that they needed not just a good preacher, but also an exceptionally able administrator to work with the staff and oversee the many ministries the church conducted. They had not fully acknowledged this before. Working with a denominational leader, Joe and the church parted ways amicably after sixteen months. There was frustration in the congregation over having to go through the process of finding a new pastor all over again, but also much greater clarity concerning the gifts they were seeking in a pastor. Joe moved to a mid-sized urban church that emphasized a rich congregational life in which the pastor was central, and he was much more satisfied there.

A pastor may also leave the ministry entirely for another field of work, as a result of a changed sense of vocation or a recognition that she is not suited for pastoral ministry. Key to such a departure will be conveying to the congregation that it is not to blame and has not failed, but that the change is necessary because of the pastor's changing sense of identity and call. On such an occasion, the congregation may feel anxious that the pastor has lost her faith and will wonder what kind of crisis could have caused such a loss. Thus, in explaining her departure, the pastor needs to assure the people that she will continue her life in the faith, simply not as a member of the clergy. As noted above, this is an important opportunity to help congregants reflect on their own sense of call.

Pastor Linda enjoyed pastoring and did her job well. She was also widely known as a skilled writer and a lover of travel. In fact, a somewhat unique aspect of her ministry had been leading trips — she called them "pilgrimages" — to various sacred Christian sites in many parts of the world. As Linda explained her decision to leave the ministry, she had been providentially made aware by a friend, "out of the blue," of an opportunity to work for a travel magazine as a writer and consultant, particularly in the area of travel based on spiritual interests. It seemed like the perfect job for her, and so she resigned her pastorate to accept it. Linda's explanation at a luncheon held in her honor shared her transition in a way that encouraged the congregation to be open to new possibilities where

their passions and opportunities intersect. Though she
was held in fond esteem by the congregation she had
served for eight years, they were able to let her go more
easily because of her explanation.

THERE ARE a variety of reasons for leaving a pastorate,
and circumstances will make some easier than others. But
in every case, the pastor's explanation of the change will
benefit everyone involved. Pastoral transitions offer the
possibility of learning and growth, of increased clarity
about who we are, what we are called to, and how we
sense our path into God's future. But these lessons can
only be learned as the pastor takes the time for sensitive
and insightful explanation.

· III ·

Thou Shalt Not Steal Away

"You shall not steal."

EXODUS 20:15

What pastor has not known excruciatingly painful moments in ministry — such as times of conflict or lack of congregational responsiveness — when he or she would like nothing so much as to "steal away to Jesus," in the words of the lovely old spiritual? Leaving a congregation with which one has enjoyed pleasant years of mutual ministry can also be a time of strong emotions, albeit more positive ones, in which it is tempting to "steal away," giving very short notice and trying to simply slip away almost unnoticed, as if it were possible to end-run all the deep feelings a pastoral transition evokes. Perhaps the most essential reason to give ample notice of a departure — three months, on average — is to allow adequate time for pastor and congregation to say goodbye with depth, honesty, and gratitude. Will it be easy? Probably not. Will it be worthwhile? Absolutely.

Some time ago, I had houseguests visiting for several days. Good food and good conversation about topics that mattered — our families, our world, our faith journeys, our dreams — made the visit a particular blessing. My sense was that we all felt known, understood, and cherished. How astonished I was, then, to get up one morning to find a note on the dining room table announcing that they had decided to head on down the road and had left to get an early start. The whole visit seemed compromised by their hasty departure, which robbed me of the opportunity to say goodbye, to say how much our time together had meant to me. Rationally, I understood their choice, as I knew they had hundreds of miles to cover. Emotionally, I felt cheated and dissatisfied.

To draw a comparison, many people say they would just as soon drop dead of a sudden, massive heart attack: "No long, drawn-out dying for me, thank you very much!" Such a preference is understandable, but there is a large and undeniable element of selfishness involved in such a wish. The aftermath through which their loved ones must make their way after such a dramatic death is riddled with the agony of words not spoken, love not expressed, forgiveness not shared. While lingering deaths are painful, to be sure, they do afford the time for meaningful farewells through which closure can be created.

Pastors who steal away leave their congregations with the same feelings and frustrations as guests who depart suddenly or loved ones who die unexpectedly. And in stealing away, they steal from their congregations. They steal the opportunity to say goodbye in meaningful encounters that provide necessary closure for everyone involved. Not only do they cheat their parishioners, but they also rob themselves of many lovely and empowering gifts congregants would willingly give if afforded the opportunity to do so. That is to say, bidding farewell is a mutual experience, one in which the pastor receives blessing as well as offers it. Being so blessed confirms the value of the ending pastorate and thereby empowers both pastor and congregation to move forward with confidence and expectancy.

Different Groups, Different Goodbyes

The Apostle Paul describes the church as being like one body with many parts. Just as each part contributes something different to the overall working of the body and just as each has its own set of needs, so each church member will have meant something different to the departing pastor. When preparing to say her goodbyes, it may be helpful for the pastor to think of the various groups of people in her congregation who deserve special attention.

In most congregations, there are people who take on the work of ministering to the minister. These folks take as their Christian vocation extending hospitality to the pastor and his family, checking in when times are tough, lending a listening ear, asking gently if the pastor is taking enough time off, quietly finding ways to help without being asked. Theirs is a work of love, and the pastor needs to make sure to thank them as part of saying goodbye. One pastor shared how he and his family hosted a dinner party for this circle of supporters during which each member of his family took turns expressing their appreciation. How blessed he was to know they would endeavor to continue their work with the next pastor of that congregation!

There are also in most congregations those to whom

the pastor feels particularly drawn — elderly members whose lifelong faithfulness has been an inspiration, ever-dependable and enthusiastic volunteers who are ready to assist in any way they can with whatever project is afoot, quiet workers who faithfully did a necessary but not particularly interesting job like folding the Sunday bulletin week after week. Call them the pillars or the plankers of the church. Just by being who they are, just by doing whatever it is they feel called to do, they have been a blessing. These, too, deserve a special goodbye, one that acknowledges their love for the church and their faithfulness over the long haul.

Another group that warrants special attention is the homebound or nursing home–bound whom the pastor has seen regularly. Often such people have a limited number of faithful visitors, and the loss of any single one is painful. And when that loss is of the one who has listened and prayed and celebrated Holy Communion with them, the loss is particularly significant. Yes, there will be another pastor, but for them that means undertaking the work of making themselves known yet again. These folks need to know that the pastor has valued his relationship with them, that they matter, and that they will be missed as individuals. Those being visited often welcome, indeed need, the opportunity to express their gratitude for the pastor's faithfulness in visitation. One pastor was brought to tears when a homebound member presented him with a copy she had carefully made of her diary entries from each day he had come to see her over the years of his pastorate, each entry detailing what they had spoken of, what they had prayed for, what they had laughed about.

One possibility for a meaningful farewell to such individuals is to celebrate Holy Communion one last time, placing special emphasis on the communion of saints. While traditions vary, most Christians believe that in the sacrament the limitations of time and space are mysteriously overcome, so that they can be in communion with the faithful of every time and place. The pastor can give the assurance that in future celebrations of the sacrament, the relationship he and the member have shared will live on.

Another group deserving of special attention are those for whom death is drawing near. Although usually few in number, members of this group may very well have been counting on the departing minister to officiate at their funeral or memorial service. This is a particularly poignant loss, which the pastor needs to acknowledge. The departing pastor can make clear that she, too, feels this loss, and that it would have been a privilege to have celebrated the life now drawing to a close. Naming things the pastor has cherished about the dying person, remembering defining stories from his or her life, offering the comfort of the faith as life comes to an end — all are key parts of saying goodbye to the dying. Here again, the sacrament of Holy Communion will most often be a welcome part of the visitation.

There will also likely be some members whom the departing pastor will not be able to visit due to their being out of town at the time of the pastoral transition. Included in this group are snowbirds, vacationers, and young people away at college or in the military. Even though they are absent from the congregation, many such people will have strong ties to the community, and therefore will have some anxiety about not being present during the leave-taking. A personal letter from the pastor to each of these members is well worth the effort. As with others, clear articulation of what the individual has meant to the pastor and the offering of a pastoral blessing will often make these letters keepsakes.

While many of these important goodbyes are best done individual by individual, it will often be the case that the pastor has worked particularly closely with certain groups in the church — governing boards, small group leaders, staff, and so forth. The departing pastor needs to meet with these groups so that she may affirm them and their work and so that they can have the opportunity to articulate what their close work in partnership with her has meant. Such gatherings, with their heartfelt give-and-take, can often bring forth much more depth of appreciation than individual interactions would afford.

Finally, the ministerial colleagues from other churches with whom one has made the journey of a pastorate need to be acknowledged and thanked. Since these are the people who understand experientially what the burdens and joys of pastoral ministry are, they have in all likelihood been valuable supports. Perhaps joint ministries or worship services have been shared over the years; perhaps study and prayer opportunities have been undertaken. Whatever the means by which collegiality has been incarnated, its worth needs to be affirmed. A luncheon or dinner together, replete with stories (and likely jokes at the departing pastor's expense!) and expressions of gratitude, will be a gift not only to the departing pastor but will also offer encouragement to the clergy who will be continuing their ministry in that community.

I well remember a colleague who had been very active

in the ministerial association of a community in which I pastored. Over the years, he and I had been part of a group of several pastors that had forged strong relationships through prayer, listening, and sharing as we encountered both personal and professional challenges. The group had laughed and cried, studied and worshiped together on many an occasion. Yet the pastor I have in mind left one midsummer for a new call without a word to any of the other group members. He just up and left, and thereby left the rest of us wondering what all we had shared together had meant to him. We found out later that he had treated his congregation similarly, giving only two weeks' notice of his departure. Some months after his move, he wrote a note saying he was sorry, but "things had just happened so quickly." Even in this note, there was no mention of what we, or our shared experience, had meant. Thereafter, the group covenanted that we would be intentional in our partings from one another.

Difficult Feelings

"I will not leave you desolate," says Jesus in the midst of his lengthy farewell discourse. How striking it is in John's Gospel that Jesus goes to such great lengths to bid his beloved community and its members farewell in a way that clarifies not only what has come to pass, but to empower them for what lies ahead! In no way does he steal away. Courageously and compassionately, Jesus takes the time to say goodbye to those he has loved, to those with whom he has made his journey, to those who will remain after his parting to continue the work of ministry. Concern, anguish, perplexity, and fear are all part of the disciples' response to Jesus' leaving. Jesus takes these seriously and speaks to them graciously. His time is spent in homes, at meals, listening and speaking. And in his farewell is guidance for our own.

In all likelihood, there will be individuals with whom it is difficult to say goodbye and come to some closure for reasons other than deep affection (more on them under the fifth commandment). But if we steal away and desert those we have loved, and who have loved us, the consequences will be unfortunate indeed. Members of the congregation will be left wondering if they did something wrong, something that alienated the departing pastor. They will question the relationship they had and wonder if the affection they perceived was an illusion. They will feel robbed of the privilege of thanking and blessing. And they may very well be cautious in receiving their next pastor out of a desire to avoid a repetition of the hurts the former pastor's callousness inflicted.

In like manner, the fleeing pastor will likely know the pangs of guilt that accompany sin, in this case the sin of theft. And the failure to say farewell openly and lovingly may haunt the building of relationships in the new ministerial context. Old wounds fester, after all, and cause increased damage where once they might have been healed with relative ease.

PRAY FOR the courage to say goodbye well to those you have loved and who have loved you. The gift of a good goodbye will bear fruit on many branches for years to come.

Thou Shalt Affirm
Thy Congregation's Ministry

*"We give thanks to God always for you all,
constantly mentioning you in our prayers,
remembering before our God and Father your
work of faith and labor of love and steadfastness
of hope."*

I THESSALONIANS 1:2-3

We live in a future-oriented time and society. Hardly do
we finish one important occasion before we are rushing
off to prepare for the next. We are all too familiar with the
mad rush from Thanksgiving to Christmas to New Year's
to Super Bowl Sunday to Valentine's Day to Holy Week
to . . . Common though it may be, both for individuals
and for churches, this is a profoundly unscriptural way to
live.

A prominent theme in Scripture, and a crucial activity
for the faith community and its members, is the act of remembering. What are the Israelites commanded to do in
Sabbath observance? "Remember that you were a slave in
the land of Egypt and the Lord your God brought you out
from there with a mighty hand and an outstretched arm"

(Deuteronomy 5:15). And when life goes well? "Remember the Lord your God, for it is God who gives you power to get wealth" (Deuteronomy 8:18). We learn to discern what God is doing through our knowledge of what God has done. We are protected from the folly of our own self-importance by remembering the One at work in and through us. Through the act of remembering, our attention is turned to the past as a way of preparing for the future.

When it comes time for a pastor to leave, in most instances the congregation will host an event to honor the departing pastor's ministry with them. Such occasions are often marked by heartfelt remembrances, humorous anecdotes, and the giving of gifts to symbolize the congregation's gratitude. But the departing pastor also has a gift to bestow in the months of leave-taking, a gift of vital importance. It is the gift of bringing to the congregation's consciousness what has been wrought over the years of his or her pastorate. One pastor put it to me this way: "As they celebrate your ministry, make sure to celebrate theirs."

There will be members of the congregation who have been present throughout the entire length of that pastorate and also those who became part of the congregation's ministry during it (and who likely do not have as broad an understanding of the church's journey). Both groups will learn more about the congregation's identity, and thus be better equipped to dream with God about who it wishes to be in days to come, through intentional remembering and recounting of what has been accomplished during the current pastor's stay.

Remembering a Pastorate

Those who have worked with the dying know how worthwhile, even transformational, an intentional remembering of an entire life can be to a dying person and to his or her loved ones. Sometimes such work is done formally, with a friend or family member asking about various seasons of the dying person's journey and audiotaping the responses; at other times it is done more informally, with various people asking the dying person to share memories, stories, and anecdotes to help put the person's life in perspective. This work helps to create a sense of gratitude for what has been, names the moments that have created meaning and value, opens the door for forgiveness to be given and received, and offers a freedom to accept what lies beyond the conclusion of this life. These same benefits can be gained when the pastor takes the time to review the congregation's life.

There are several ways this review and affirmation can proceed. A wise first step is for the pastor to sit down with some active and insightful church members — including, if possible, folks who were part of bringing the pastor to the church — who have been present for the duration of the pastorate to discuss questions such as:

How are we different today from how we were when the pastor came?

What accomplishments in ministry are we most grateful for?

What challenges have we overcome and what did we learn from those situations?

What do we wish we might have done had time and resources allowed?

Prior to this discussion, the pastor can review annual reports and peruse church newsletters to jog his own memory about what has come to pass. The length of the pastorate and the age of the pastor can make this work especially important!

The information garnered from these endeavors can be shared with the congregation in a variety of ways. Pastor Judith took the time to organize the remembrances around various aspects of her congregation's life, and then, over her last two months, wrote a series of articles in her church's biweekly newsletter summarizing the accomplishments. In an article on worship, she noted the addition of healing services, the development of a series of fine arts concerts, and the integration of Taizé-style music into morning services. Addressing congregational care, she wrote of the expanded work and training of deacons for visitation ministry, the creation of an ongoing bereavement group, and the development of an intercessory prayer ministry by the homebound for the church's ministry. When she wrote about missions, she rejoiced in the congregation's commitment to Habitat for Humanity and highlighted several youth mission trips. And in the Christian education piece, she celebrated the many small study and fellowship groups, particularly a group for men, which had been established and now flourished.

By using the newsletter as her means of communication, she ensured that all the congregation, those who attended regularly as well as those who did not for whatever reason, were included in the review. And Judith found she got more comments on these articles than on almost anything else she had written over the years! Clearly, she had done a valuable work.

The Reverend Andrew took a different, but also effective, approach to the task of leaving his congreation with words of encouragement. His strengths lay in biblical study and teaching, as well as in creative preaching. Knowing his strengths, he pondered the information he had gathered and offered it to the congregation in the form of a "pastoral letter" sermon modeled after Paul's epistles. This he did on a Sunday a month before his departure date and in conjunction with a church potluck that afforded time for congregational response.

The sermon began much like Paul's Letter to the Philippians, with exuberant gratitude for the congregation's members and work. Andrew then went on to detail the many specific examples of how the congregation had grown in faith and service over the years. The middle section of the sermon expressed Andrew's deep gratitude for the congregation's support and understanding, particularly for its ministry to him when he had undergone major surgery some years previously. And it concluded with an exhortation to keep the faith, to run the race as well and faithfully as the congregation had done in days gone by, and to be open and expectant of the new work God would yet do in and through the church.

At the potluck, members were invited to speak in response to Andrew's message. From the remarks shared, it was clear that the congregation felt known and valued. And members left that day with a sense of empowerment for the future they would know with a new pastor and their God.

Pastor Mike served a church that was blessed with a member who meticulously kept photographs, newspaper articles, and church publications about virtually every congregational activity. Working with this woman, Mike created an extensive display that went all the way around the walls of the church's fellowship room. This provided a poignant backdrop for his farewell dinner and served to trigger all manner of detailed recollections of the life Mike and the congregation had shared over his twelve years of pastoral leadership. The faithful recorder of church life also recorded this event in a short essay that articulated the church's identity as it had unfolded over those years.

While such approaches are most pleasant when the concluding ministry has been fruitful and satisfying, they are also helpful when the pastorate has been marked by difficult moments and conflict. Whether in written, spoken, or visual form (or some combination thereof), the pastor can give clarity about the struggles engaged over the years and what growth, painful though it may have been, has been wrought through them. To the pastor, this process may feel somewhat akin to "the painful letter" that Paul speaks of in 2 Corinthians, and it is a process that must be undertaken with a careful balancing of honesty and compassion.

As Pastor Lois looked back over her eleven-year pastorate in a middle-sized church, the image that came to mind was that of a roller coaster. Two incidents, separated by three years, had wracked her congregation — the coming to light of sexual abuse committed by a previous pastor, and the surprising and bitter divorce of the most active and admired couple in the church. (The latter grew so acrimonious that one ex-spouse accused the other of adultery during the announcement time during worship!) Between and around these two crises, the church had established a domestic assault shelter, dramatically increased its church school, and remodeled its sanctuary. As she was preparing to leave, Lois decided that the worst choice she could make would be to adopt a Pollyannaish approach to the review of her pastorate, one that glossed over, denied, or trivialized the very real and lingering pain the congregation had known.

Lois chose to write a long letter that was mailed to every member of the church. Entitled "Knowing God on the High Roads and Low Roads," her letter reviewed the paths that she and the congregation had traveled, and named with joy the congregation's several accomplishments even as it also sought to name how God had been at work to comfort, sustain, and heal the congregation. In her conclusion, she specifically called upon her people not to remember selectively, lest they miss the work of God in every season of life, lest they think God was only present and at work when life was going well. The letter confirmed the important theological lessons Lois had sought to draw out in the midst of the two crises, but which had not been heard at the time because of the emotional turmoil the congregation was experiencing.

Lois found herself receiving letters in return. Thank-you notes, some that said they would be sealed with tears of gratitude, arrived during her last weeks. And at her farewell dinner, one member seemed to speak for all when he said that from Lois he had learned what it meant to wait upon the Lord for the healing we are meant to have in Christ.

In addition to pointing out what the congregation does well, what it has accomplished, how it has grown, and what it has learned, it is important for the departing pastor to express gratitude for the care he or she has received from the congregation. This can be done in a sermon, as Andrew did as part of his pastoral epistle; through a newsletter article or congregational letter; or as part of comments shared in the context of a farewell event. This expression of gratitude is important not only as a means of acknowledging the significance of both giver and gift, but also as a gentle reminder to the congregation that it has an obligation to care for its pastor, whoever that may be. Just as some church members mistakenly believe God exists to serve them rather than vice versa, so some may see their relationship with the pastor as analogously one-way. Thus, the departing pastor's "thank you" not only graciously closes the circle of giving and receiving, but also helps pave the way for the congregation to be in healthy and mutual relationship with the next pastor.

AFFIRMATION OF the congregation's ministry is a crucial task in the months of saying goodbye. Done with pastoral insight and sensitivity, this summation work will help clarify the congregation's identity by specifically naming dimensions of its shared life. Without this work, the congregation may flounder in its sense of calling, or worse, drift back into old patterns the pastor has labored to help it overcome. Creative and faithful remembering of all that has come to pass under the Spirit's guidance will not only help the congregation move forward with confidence and clarity, but will also free the pastor to embrace whatever new path is opening into the future.

• V •

Thou Shalt Try to Mend Fences

"God . . . through Christ reconciled us to himself, and gave us the ministry of reconciliation."

2 CORINTHIANS 5:18

The Apostle Paul may have been able to "become all things to all people" (1 Corinthians 9:22), but most pastors are not similarly gifted. Unless a pastor has been content with relationships no deeper than a puddle in a parking lot, he or she will have had relationships with people in the congregation that have been marked by conflict and negative feelings. These are usually among the aspects of a concluding ministry that pastors are not loath to leave behind! While most relationships with church members will have been good and nourishing, it is inevitable that there will also have been individuals with whom pastors have had personality conflicts, significant differences of opinion on anything from theology to repaving the parsonage driveway, or hurt feelings from words spoken in the midst of personal crisis.

While it may be tempting to "shake off the dust from your feet as you leave that town" (Matthew 10:14) with regard to such folks, this is not in the best interest of either pastor or parishioner, to say nothing of one's Christian responsibility to work through such difficulties. There may also be the temptation to speak words bitten back for years, to fire a parting shot in a conflict at a time when there is little chance for retaliation. Yielding to such temptations — and many departing pastors do, unfortunately — will tarnish the pastor's reputation and elicit feelings of guilt when the momentary satisfaction of the skewering remark, scathingly delivered, passes. Without doubt, the germane text is Matthew 5:23-24: "If you are offering your gift at the altar, and there remember that your brother or sister has something against you, leave your gift there before the altar and go; first be reconciled to your brother or sister."

Wrestling with Hogs

In the closing months of a pastorate, after one's departure has been announced, the better part of pastoral wisdom is to compile a list of those individuals with whom one has unresolved conflict or antagonistic feelings. After taking adequate deep breaths and praying for the gift of a gracious demeanor, the departing pastor should start arranging to meet personally with each person on the list. It is best to hold these meetings on neutral territory — say at a restaurant for coffee or a meal together — rather than in the pastor's study or at the parishioner's home. Meeting on neutral ground will assist in deemphasizing the power the pastor has in her study or in her professional role as pastoral visitor.

The content of each meeting will vary according to the specific nature of the conflict with the parishioner. In some cases, the pastor may wish to express regret for the precipitating incident. In others, reconciliation may come naturally; there may even be laughter over the rigidity with which both parties stuck to their guns over an issue that, in retrospect, did not have nearly the importance each chose to attach to it. Sometimes, hopefully rarely, the parishioner may wish to resume the dispute, and here the pastor must simply acknowledge his or her regret over the original incident and bring the meeting to as prompt and gracious a close as possible, offering his best wishes for the parishioner's continued journey in faith. The old warning about wrestling with hogs applies here: Don't do it. You can't win, it makes the hogs happy, and you end up dirty.

No matter the parishioner's response, however, the pastor will do well to attempt on a personal scale the kind of good goodbye that I described in the preceding chapter. That is, to the extent possible, the goal of such meetings is to affirm the parishioner's faith and contributions to the church's ministry. Proverbs 15:1 tells us that "a soft answer turns away wrath," and often prayerfully seeking a gracious spirit will lead to surprising and satisfying mendings. And if mending is not possible, then at least there may be peace at having done what could be done.

Pastor Jake was well-known for his candid opinions. Many in his congregation were drawn to the clarity this straightforwardness lent his leadership; a few disagreed with him in terms nearly as strong as his own. Under Jake's leadership, the congregation had played a significant role in the development of a transitional housing facility for homeless individuals and families. The project had placed large demands on the congregation for volunteer time and was constantly struggling financially. Alex was a church member who had opposed the project right from its inception precisely because of its volunteer and financial requirements, which he viewed as excessive. He had believed that the project would potentially undermine other longstanding community services the congregation had supported — a soup kitchen, an emergency food pantry, and a clothing distribution center among them.

In that last month of Jake's pastorate, he and Alex met for breakfast at a local restaurant. The meeting began tentatively, with chitchat about Jake's impending move. After a little while, Jake said, "Alex, I wanted to get together to acknowledge that you were right. The housing project has consumed an awful lot of our church's resources, more than I had thought it would. I do feel it was, and is, needed, but it has proven to be a strain."

The two men were quiet for a while, and then Alex said with a small grin, "I'm trying to resist the temptation to say 'I told you so.' But, you know, Jake, I don't think it should be abandoned, now that it's here."

"Well, what do you think needs to happen?" asked Jake with some surprise and curiosity.

"Well, as an engineer, I think we need to look at our whole system of trying to meet the needs of these marginalized folks. All that we're doing just sprung up as needs arose. People were hungry; we tried to feed them. People needed clothes; we tried to provide them. Just like Jesus said, in Matthew, I think. But we never looked very much at how these folks' needs overlapped, or how we could coordinate our responses. You see, we had this pastor who was really good at seeing a need and getting us to jump in with a response." They both laughed. "So, when the new pastor comes, I'm going to suggest — no, I'm going to offer to lead — such an effort. And I'm going to try to get the other like-minded churches and pastors involved, too. Maybe even some of the unlike-minded!"

After a moment, Jake said, "That's a great idea. I wish we'd done it long ago. You're right, my enthusiasm and can-do-ism doesn't always leave much room for that kind of systems thinking."

"Well," said Alex, "I was too busy fighting you, trying to stop you, to take the time to come up with some alternatives."

"But now you have, and your idea is more than worthwhile," said Jake. After breakfast, they shook hands. And then they had a mild, good-humored argument over who was going to pick up the check. "I guess we'll always have disagreements about something!" Jake concluded with a smile.

But achieving a measure of reconciliation takes two willing parties, and not all parishioners are like Alex. Pastor Deb asked a member named Fred, with whom she had often been at odds over the years of her pastorate, to have lunch with her. He agreed, but then showed up so late that Deb had begun to wonder if he had decided not to come. Finally, he arrived, thrust himself into a chair, announced he would just have coffee, and asked, "What's this all about anyway, Deb?"

"Well, Fred, as I've been getting ready to move, it occurred to me that you and I had been at each other more than a few times. We disagreed about adding the contemporary service, about installing the elevator, about the Christmas Eve service, about . . ."

"And sponsoring that missionary in Honduras, and the landscaping," interrupted Fred.

"Yes, exactly," said Deb, well aware of anger rising within her. She took a breath to compose herself, quickly asked God for grace in the moment, and then said, "What this is about, Fred, is my wanting to let you know before I leave that, in spite of all those disagreements, I value your faithfulness to our church. You're in worship every Sunday. You've served on any number of committees and are always prepared. You volunteer to help out most anytime, anywhere, for any task. You've hung in there in spite of how differently we see things. I want you to know that I truly appreciate that. And I thank God for your faithfulness."

Fred was silent for a few moments. Then, he said, "Well, thanks, I guess. I just hope our new minister won't have so many cockamamie ideas and want to go off in all sorts of weird directions. Is that all you wanted to say? You could have just called me on the phone!" And with that, he looked about, huffed, got up, nodded at Deb, and left. There was no debate over who would pay the bill. Deb finished her lunch and was able to head back to the office with a smile knowing she had done what she could, and that Fred would always be Fred.

The Benefits of Reconciliation

There are several benefits of such intentional efforts at reconciliation. At the rudimentary level, no one, neither pastor nor parishioner, enjoys going through life nagged by the what-ifs of unresolved conflicts. Even where the brokenness cannot be fully mended, no matter how good the intentions to do so, the effort made affords a sense of closure that allows easier movement into the future.

For parishioners, it can be a blessing to know that they have been heard and that some, if not all, of their contributions to the faith community's life have been valued by the pastor. If this appreciation is not given and received, the parishioner may well project the unresolved feelings onto all pastors generally, and onto the next pastor specifically. In other words, unresolved conflict with one pastor may be transferred to another.

In one church I served, a parishioner approached me shortly after my arrival. He was so similar in demeanor to Pastor Deb's parishioner Fred that I will call him Fred the Second. Although I had previously met him only briefly as he left church after worship one Sunday, I sensed strong antagonism from the moment he sat down in my office. He opened our conversation bluntly: "I understand you've already changed the board's docket all around." I acknowledged that I had added a time for the sharing of personal joys and concerns, but was able to resist commenting that I did not consider this "changing the docket all around."

Fred II continued, "That'll probably be just the beginning of things you'll start changing. That's what you pastors do, change everything around. Just like the last reverend." I gently tried to explain my approach to initiating change with a new congregation, suggesting that I would be taking time to get a sense of how things currently were and how they had been done in the past. When I didn't bite on his invitation to wrestle, Fred II soon left, saying, "I'll see you around."

I asked my secretary what that might have been about — in particular, if my predecessor had taken some action that had particularly annoyed Fred II. She thought for a moment and then recalled that Fred II's mother had given a pulpit Bible to the church many years before. My predecessor had decided, with the board's support, to start using a new Bible translation in worship, and so the church had purchased a new pulpit Bible. In consultation with the board, that minister had offered either to give the old Bible to Fred II's family or to have it displayed as part of a group of historical items from the church's life. Although Fred II took the Bible, he made it clear he did not like that "it wasn't good enough for the church anymore."

I do not know what efforts at reconciliation my predecessor had attempted, if any. Given Fred II's demeanor, they may well have been rebuffed. What became clear to me in that interaction is that the lack of reconciliation made me suspect in Fred II's eyes almost before I arrived. As a kindness, then, to one's successor, the departing pastor should attempt to reconcile differences with angry or disaffected members so that the next pastor may have as even a start as possible.

IN THE LONG RUN, it is always more satisfying to bless than to curse. Blessing opens the possibility of being freed so that everyone — parishioner, departing pastor, and incoming pastor — will have a better chance of moving into the next phase of ministry unencumbered by the unexamined, unacknowledged, or unforgiven hurts of the past. We are human; we are imperfect; we are frail. And so it is that some hurt may not be resolved, some relationships may not be reconciled. But the effort to do so, to affirm with honesty and grace what can be affirmed, will afford benefits even when done imperfectly or without complete success.

· VI ·

Thou Shalt Help Thy Successor Have a Good Beginning

"Write the vision, make it plain upon tablets, so he may run who reads it."

HABAKKUK 2:2

Here are two questions for the departing pastor to ponder: What do you know now that you wish you had known when you started the pastorate you are now leaving? As an act of gracious collegiality and Christian fellowship, why not share this information with your successor?

Leaving a good and clear set of tracks for one's successor will not only benefit him; it will also help to minimize the inevitable loss of momentum the congregation will experience during the pastoral transition. Two items, a map and a history, will prove most useful. An old Arab proverb says that if you don't know where you're going, any road will take you there. Having a clear sense of where the congregation has been prior to his arrival on the scene can play a big role in helping a new pastor figure out which direction to go.

The history should include a wide range of helpful information, and it should be provided in written form. Depending on the situation, and particularly the level of conflict that has marked the concluding pastorate, it is often wise for the departing pastor to deliver this information directly to the new one in order to insure confidentiality. The documents should include an overview of what has been accomplished during the departing pastor's sojourn with the congregation, as well as some indication of what might have been the focal areas of ministry were the pastor not leaving.

The new pastor should also be aware of the terrain he is about to enter; this is where the map comes in. An assessment of the congregation's strengths and weaknesses will be necessary, and it may also be helpful for the departing pastor to consider sharing the same information about himself. The departing pastor will most likely be in a good position to identify both longstanding traditions and persistent struggles that have shaped the congregation's life.

In order to help one's successor get off to a good start in taking on the more personal aspects of a pastorate, such as ministering to the critically ill, the recently bereaved, those who have lost their jobs, and so forth, the map should also include a list of these individuals and what their particular needs are. The new pastor will, of course, have his own approach to meeting the congregation pastorally, but this list will help him know where it will be most helpful to begin.

Pastor Nancy had come into her congregation after her predecessor had left quite suddenly following some fairly intense conflict for which he bore considerable responsibility. The church's secretary of many years had also resigned at that time as an act of loyalty to the departed pastor. Furthermore, much of the church's life and records were in disarray. Congregational life had withered to the point that it was all the church could manage to hold worship on Sunday.

Having labored long and hard to bring order, pattern, and renewed energy to the chaos she had inherited, she was determined to provide her successor with the sort of information that would have simplified her own transition several years before. Nancy developed a packet of materials, for her successor's eyes only, which included the following:

- a copy of a published church history done some years earlier for the congregation's centennial celebration;
- her own detailed account of her ministry, which had included a major building project, expansion of the music program, and the development of an active mission partnership with a church in Nigeria;
- a copy of the current year's budget;
- her evaluation of the congregation's strengths (worship innovation and mission) and weaknesses (persistent struggles in offering Christian education for all ages) and her own strengths (preaching and pastoral care) and weaknesses (overcommitment to denominational work and impatience with administrative detail);
- a list of every family that had experienced a death or a serious illness in the preceding year;
- a list of those who had joined the church within the preceding year;
- a schedule of annual events that were absolutely

central (i.e., to be tampered with only at great peril) to the church's tradition (a spring pig roast, an annual community Thanksgiving dinner, a women's collectibles sale and accompanying lasagna dinner);
- a description of cooperative programs with other churches (food bank, vacation Bible school, CROP Walk, and special worship services);
- a list of community boards and functions of which she had been a part (the hospital's community advisory board, high school band boosters, assistant soccer coach) and those she had not (Rotary Club, praying at city council meetings);
- a description of issues confronting the community that would affect church members (such as an upcoming millage vote to fund the construction of a new middle school);
- and, finally, the names of her physician, dentist, chiropractor, real estate agent, and car mechanic!

Nancy also made clear in a cover letter that she would call the new pastor one (and only one) time to see if he had any questions, and included her new phone number in case he ever wished to sound her out about any aspect of the church's life. The new pastor called her twice: once to say how deeply grateful he was for this informational packet; and a second time to ask her advice about whether he was reading a certain pastoral situation accurately. The pastoral transition went smoothly, and the congregation retained a high level of functioning throughout the change.

It took Nancy quite bit of time during her busy final weeks to put all this information together, but having finished the task, she found she had also done herself a favor in helping the incoming pastor. The very work of gathering the information and reflecting on it had given her a profound sense of closure as well as gratitude for the years she had spent in this pastorate. In fact, she felt so good about the project that she told her husband that it would have been worthwhile even if she had been followed by a "reinvent the wheel"-type pastor who wanted to find out everything on his own.

Of course, different denominations have different procedures for handling pastoral transitions. Some are firmly committed to having a specially trained interim pastor in between permanent pastors, particularly in congregations that have experienced significant conflict. Other denominations prefer to appoint a new pastor who begins his work the Sunday following his predecessor's last Sunday. Regardless, an informational packet will be valuable. If used by an interim pastor, it will enable that individual, whose tenure is usually relatively brief, to hit the ground running; and if it is honest and detailed in its descriptions of what the congregation has gone through, it will help the interim focus her skills where they are most needed. For the permanent pastor, such an informational packet will be an invaluable aid as he seeks to comprehend the longer-standing patterns of congregational life and to begin to understand the context in which his new ministry will come to pass.

If the departing pastor thinks it would prove helpful, the information packet could be shared with a denominational official as well, as a means of strengthening the larger church's understanding of the particular congregation.

Often denominational officials are the ones to whom

congregations turn when various problems arise. Having a broader picture of the congregation's life on hand will be helpful when the intensity of a conflict threatens to obscure the larger context within which the problem is occurring.

SOME PASTORS may not wish to undertake the work of leaving tracks, believing that if their successor learns the congregation on his or her own, the lesson secured will be of more value. On the other hand, it may be nothing more than laziness or petulance ("I had to find my way, let her find hers!") that explains why some may choose not to do this work. Failure to take the time to help the new pastor, for whatever reason, is inconsiderate, harmful to the congregation, and can leave the departing pastor with a sense of incompletion. Leaving well is about blessing those who remain and those who will follow, and the gift of detailed documentation will be a blessing to everyone involved in the pastoral transition.

Thou Shalt Be Gentle with Thyself

"You shall love your neighbor as yourself."

MATTHEW 22:39B

The first six commandments have proposed a considerable amount of hard labor for the departing pastor — explanations to give, farewell calls to make, histories to write, instructions to leave. And all the while, many of the regular demands of ministry will continue unabated — emergent pastoral needs, committee meetings, and, of course, what Calvin Didier once termed "the haunting, sweet agony of next Sunday's sermon." Unsurprisingly, the pastor's self-care is the thing most likely to get lost in the midst of all these claims on his or her time and energy. We can become so busy meeting others' needs — our parishioners', our successor's, our family's (more on them in the next chapter) — that attentiveness to our ongoing and essential needs is easily lost in the frenzied shuffle of the eschatological days of a pastorate.

There is a striking assumption in the passage from Leviticus that Jesus chooses as his summary of the last six commandments: that we will, and do, love ourselves. In our day and culture, obsession with self is regrettably and sinfully common. But often, despite this obsession, or perhaps because of it, there is a lack of the healthy valuing and caring for that we need. Amidst the normal rigors of parish ministry, not to mention the extra demands of a pastoral change, far too many pastors neglect caring for themselves. Thus not only do they fail to model appropriate self-care to their congregations; they often fall victim to burnout. And ending a pastorate exhausted is no way to prepare for a pastoral transition.

I have elsewhere proposed a biblical approach to self-care that is intended to empower ministry and model faithfulness,* and I will not repeat that material here. But it is important to remember that times of transition greatly increase the stress of the already enormously stressful vocation that is parish ministry. Thus, faithful care of all dimensions of the self — physical, emotional, intellectual, spiritual — is crucial. That means taking time to exercise, to see friends, to receive graciously, to read, to pursue hobbies, to pray, to meet with a mentor or spiritual director or counselor. Making a de facto decision that one is simply too busy for these activities is a sure way to guarantee one will lack the resources needed to make a good pastoral transition.

Pastor Anna could feel her energy waning as she struggled to meet the many demands the last weeks of her pastorate had placed on her. When she finally took some time to reflect with a colleague about how she was handling

---

* See my *Ten Commandments for Pastors New to a Congregation* (Grand Rapids, Michigan: Eerdmans Publishing Company, 2003), pp. 48-58.

her departing, she realized she had, some weeks prior, stopped taking her dog for a daily two mile walk before supper — which meant she didn't sleep as well at night which meant she slept in a bit longer in the morning which meant she didn't eat breakfast which meant she ate a carbohydrate-laden muffin mid-morning which meant she felt tired in the afternoon which meant she did not take her dog for a walk. . . . And so it went, day after day. This pattern is a clear example of how failing to do those things that we know enable us to function at our best is self-defeating and, unfortunately, self-perpetuating. By realizing that so much of how she felt and functioned depended on taking her dog for a walk, Anna was able to get herself back on track, and her renewed commitment to self-care increased the energy she needed for her farewell work.

Another important discipline for self-care, particularly during the transition time, is self-forgiveness. Not all the tasks I have set forth in these commandments are going to get done, or they will not get done as well as we would like. There will be people with whom we don't get the time for closure we would like. In spite of our best efforts, there will be loose ends that our successor will just have to deal with. There may be unresolved conflict. This is not an excuse for falling prey to sloth, that most pernicious of the Seven Deadly Sins. It is to say we can only do the best we can, and then submit that best effort to the congregation and to God as our farewell offering. God will forgive us. Our congregation will most likely forgive us. To complete this trinity, we must also forgive ourselves for what doesn't get done. Failing to do so will lead us into retirement or a new pastorate haunted by whispers of, "I really should have . . ."

VII

A question that often arises in the context of leaving is what to do with any unused vacation time or continuing education leave. If the understanding with the congregation or governing board regarding the latter is that it is to be used to benefit the congregation being served, it may be best not to use it and to consider any associated funds as a donation to the church. But vacation time is another matter. Trying to squeeze in one's remaining vacation days during the last busy weeks of a pastorate usually disrupts the flow of leave-taking. A common and wise practice is to set a date for the conclusion of one's pastorate, and then to stay on the payroll after that date for the duration of one's remaining vacation time.

This is a particularly wise choice when one is moving to a new field of service, as it allows valuable down time in the midst of the transition. Finishing up in one church on one Sunday and beginning in the next the following Sunday is the pattern in some denominations, but if vacation time, even a little of it, can be arranged in between the two calls, a better ending and a better beginning are likely to result.

Using vacation time in this way can provide much-needed time with one's family; it can also allow time for the transitioning pastor to dream of what is to come. Such dreaming is wonderfully valuable, but really should be done on the pastor's own time, not on that of the congregation being left. This is a task not for the last weeks of a pastorate, but only for after the last day of service, if at all possible. One congregation was more than a little perturbed when its phone bill revealed that the former pastor had made many long calls to the community to which he was moving. It wasn't the dollar amount of the bill that was irksome; it was the sense that he had actually left in time and spirit long before he was actually off the payroll.

Vacation dreaming can allow a pastor in transition to ponder many important questions: What have I learned during this pastorate that I want to incorporate into my new ministry? What patterns from my last call do I hope not to fall into in the new one? What disciplines will I cultivate to sustain me? What might be possible with the new congregation — by virtue of location, history, gifts, resources — that wasn't possible with the previous congregation? What am I excited about, within and without the church, in the new context? To whom will I look for collegiality and support? What deficiencies might I be bringing to this new work, and how am I going to address them? What are going to be the crucial questions I need to ask in the new work, and to whom should these be addressed? All of these questions may be part of shaping the dream the pastor hopes to bring to concrete reality in the ministry soon to begin. In some cases, they may give rise to quite specific, written plans for how the new ministry will begin.

Another aspect important to self-care during a transition has to do with what time of year is best to make a move. Not a few pastors have shared with me how it seemed like a great idea to leave right after either Christmas or Easter. That way, their reasoning went, they could go out on a high note and enter the new pastorate during a slower season of the church year. Actually, and regrettably, what most often happens when transitions are so timed is that the transitional demands laid on top of the demands of Christmas or Easter preparations leave the pastor terribly exhausted, with little or no energy left to face not only a new pastorate, but also the rigors of moving a household and family.

Some hierarchical denominations move all their transitioning pastors at the same time of year, usually, and wisely, in the summer months when congregational life has slowed down a bit. In other denominations, where the pastor has a greater measure of say in the timing of a move, summer is also a wise choice. If a pastor can set aside the egotism that says, "I can go from one major stressful event (departing immediately after a major church festival) to another major stressful event (engaging all the newness and complexity of a new pastorate) without difficulty," she will be much better off, and her family will be, too. And both the old and new congregations will reap the benefits of having the pastor's best energies available to the meet the demands of the situation.

Transitioning pastors need always to remember the essential truth that change causes stress. And it's a direct correlation: the more change, the more stress. It is that clear and simple. We need to recall our limitations in coping with stress, doing all that is necessary to insure that our stress management capabilities are at their best. Acceptance of our limitations and commitment to self-care are nowhere more needed in pastoral ministry than in the time of leaving a congregation.

• VIII •

Thou Shalt Attend to Thy Family

*"Is there anyone among you who, if your child
asks for bread, will give a stone? Or if the child
asks for a fish, will give a snake?"*

MATTHEW 7:9-10

The decision to move impacts pastors' families as profoundly as it does pastors themselves. Most likely family members will share in the range of emotions — from anger to sadness to excitement to regret to anxiety, and most everything in between — moving within the pastor during a time of transition. There will be stress for each family member as their frendships are stretched by distance. Spouses may resent being uprooted from jobs they enjoy, or they may be glad to explore new opportunities. Children may be dismayed to be uprooted from a familiar school and church, and all the activities — music, drama, sports, clubs, youth groups — associated with them, or they may be excited about the adventures to come. If the pastorate being left was marked by conflict, the whole family may breathe a sigh of relief about the leaving. In other situations, family members may be angry at having to leave behind much that has brought them happiness, identity, and security.

The dynamics of the transition can also be more difficult by virtue of the truth that the pastor cannot pastor his or her own family. To try to add that role to those of spouse and parent is to wear far too many hats, probably none of them well. Nonetheless, he or she can listen and support, all the while being attentive to their needs. The pastor must never allow the work of seeking closure with the congregation to become an excuse for ignoring his or her family's needs. The pastor whose priority list reads "God, family, church" will always, in times of stability and in times of transition, be more effective than the one whose list is "God, church, family." In focusing on the vocations of spouse and parent, the departing pastor who has a family must take care not to assume that all members of the family are reacting to the change in the same way. Spouses will likely respond differently from children; children will likely respond differently from one another depending on what the change appears to cost or offer them.

If the departing pastor is married, his or her spouse will certainly have been involved in the decision to move, hopefully providing prayerful support and a listening ear as the pastor wrestles with the decision. But once the decision is made, the shoe is on the other foot. Now it is the pastor's turn, in the role of husband or wife, to provide the prayerful support and listening ear, as the spouse works through the challenges caused by the pastor's decision. All manner of questions may arise: Will there be a job as satisfying as the one I now have? Is this a time when I can try something different, like going back to school or being a stay-at-home parent? How will I maintain contact with the close friends I've made here? How will I find time to take care of all the details of getting school and medical records changed? What if the kids don't like the new place?

Pastor Naomi said the two most important commitments she made during the last months of her pastorate were to take time every week to go out to dinner with her husband, and to sit with one of her two kids for half an hour each night, alternating nights between them. During these special times, she mostly listened and held hands and cried, and sometimes dreamed. It was painful at times to realize how much her decision was costing her family. Soon, though, it seemed as if her family might be able to handle the transition more smoothly. Her husband was contemplating taking a few months off, even from seeking a new job, to be as available as possible to their children while they adjusted to a new setting. Also, her older daughter confided to her that she was discouraged by the changes she saw in some of her friends as they approached high school, and she recognized that a new school might offer new possibilities. Naomi's younger daughter, on the other hand, was angry and afraid about having to leave behind friends, her beloved fourth-grade teacher, and the only home she had ever known.

Between pastorates, Naomi was able to take almost a full month off, which created time in which she could focus primarily on being a wife and mother. This vacation time greatly eased the transition, as it helped everyone to release, and to give thanks for, the past, and to begin to be open to a new future. She continued to listen as deeply as she could to each member of her family, particularly to her younger daughter, as they made their way through the transition. And when they arrived at the new parish, she was surprised at how readily her family embraced the new situation. Even her younger daughter was able to see new possibilities in their new community and home (particularly as she got to decorate her new room just as she liked).

Out of his experience in moving with children, a pastor colleague of Naomi's gave her some wise counsel concerning her children: that she make sure not to tell them that the move was something God had decided and about which she had no choice. This sort of buck-passing evasion of both responsibility and accountability could dramatically impact the children's faith, in the short and the long term, if they were to transfer frustrations with their mother onto God. The "God made me do it" explanation does not speak well of either God or the pastor! Instead, the pastor should share how he or she is seeking to be faithful to God's leading, acknowledging how this can hurt loved ones but hopefully can open the possibility for growing in faith through the experience.

Pastor Nathan's wife and three children were all frustrated and angry about his decision to move after a ten-year pastorate. "Why couldn't we have moved before I got my job?" his wife asked dismally. "Why couldn't we have moved before I was in the middle of high school or after I had graduated?" his daughter wailed. "Why do I have to leave my soccer team after we did so well this year?" asked his middle-school-aged son, angrily attempting to kick the ball through the garage door. "Why do I have to leave my friends?" his sad and puzzled youngest son asked, speaking for all of them. Nathan felt he had to have adequate answers for all these questions; he felt almost unbearably guilty when no such answers were to be found.

Nathan and his family went into family counseling during the last several weeks of his leave-taking. It was a difficult and sometimes painful process, for even though it defused some of the family's emotional intensity, it also raised some significant communication issues and assumptions about roles in the family. The family agreed to continue in counseling once the move was accomplished, and this proved to be helpful both in the stress of the transition as well as in changing relational patterns. A therapeutic environment gave everyone a safe place, and thereby hope, as they moved through their many changes.

If the pastor and his or her family have not had blood relatives living nearby, it may well be the case that friends, both from within and without the congregation, have served as a surrogate extended family. As these people will share the sense of loss the pastor's family is experiencing, it is important for both family and friends-who-are-like-family to ritualize the parting. It can help to be creative in finding ways to bring these people together to share food, tell stories, and give and receive gifts. One pastor and his wife invited all the couples with whom they had regularly shared meals with each bringing their all-time favorite dish. This called to mind many, many stories, and the group was able to share words of appreciation and to express what the friendships had meant over the years. Another pastor and his children carefully designed cards for the family's closest friends, each with a personalized note ("I like you because . . .") on one side and the family's new address and phone number on the other.

VIII

If all this is important for the pastor with a family, it is absolutely essential for the single pastor, whose friends often are cherished as surely as any family. Here, perhaps even more than with families, clarity and honesty about not only what the relationships have meant, but also about the intentionality that will be necessary to sustain them, will mark the empowering farewell.

Pastor Irene had been widowed young and remained single, and over a period of years she had gathered to herself a group of three women friends — two married, one single like Irene — who were members of her church. They called themselves "the Sisters of Sustenance," and originally, the name had simply expressed their shared love and habit of finding unique places to eat in the city where they lived. Over time, their bond grew into deep, committed friendship; they counted on one another for support and comfort in any situation, no matter how grave — relationship struggles, job changes, aging parents' needs, a miscarriage, illness. They also celebrated birthdays together with great joy, determined to see each one as a triumph of maturing rather than as another year of aging. They had vacationed together twice, once going on a cruise, once renting a lakeside cottage for a week.

From Irene's first stirrings of restlessness, the Sisters of Sustenance had dialogued with her about seeking a new call. Well before Irene's last day, the group had already committed itself to a future vacation rendezvous. But then one member asked Irene if their continued friendship would decrease the likelihood of Irene forming new friendships in her new community. At first, Irene responded with a cheery, "Oh, you know. 'Make new friends, but keep the old.'" But then, more thoughtfully, she said, "You're right.

I count on you so much for regular support, week in and week out, that I really must remember to be open to welcoming the new friends God will place in my path. Talking to you on the phone, sending and receiving cards and e-mails, and taking annual vacations will be wonderful. But what I've learned from you is that I'll always need some women like you very present in my life."

In that moment, Irene began a realistic assessment of how her friendships could and could not be carried into her new life. This is a crucial task for the pastor, and for each member of the pastor's family. Some relationships can be continued, but none can remain unchanged. And openness and expectancy of new relationships emerging is born of honesty about what is being lost.

IN RECENT YEARS, some of the expectations placed upon pastors' families have been relaxed, due in part to the increase in number of women pastors in many denominations, and of single pastors and second-career pastors in all denominations. Pastoral spouses in many denominations are no longer assumed always to be female, and even in those where they are, they are not automatically assigned to leadership in congregational women's groups. Likewise, it is not as onerous as it once was to be a "PK," a preacher's kid, who is held to a behavioral standard higher than that of other children. These changes are healthy, but because of them pastors' families are not likely to go meekly and without complaint wherever the family's allegedly most important member chooses. And the crucial importance of friends to single pastors means attention to their needs at the time of a pastoral transition is like unto that of families.

To be faithful to these relationships in the midst of transition, the pastor must lay aside his or her professional role in order to be spouse, parent, and friend, and to give all the time and honest interaction needed to meet and understand the challenges imposed by the change. Attending to the needs of the congregation is important spiritually and professionally. Attending to the needs of family members and friends is the stuff of abundant life itself.

• IX •

Thou Shalt (Usually) Stay Away Once Thou Hast Left

"But Lot's wife, behind him, looked back, and she became a pillar of salt."

GENESIS 19:26

There is no universal policy that dictates the appropriate relationship between a pastor and his or her former parish. Some denominations strictly limit contact, permitting neither conversation with parishioners about church life nor functioning in any pastoral capacity (such as officiating at weddings or funerals) except upon explicit invitation of the governing board or current pastor. Others set no limits at all on these interactions, trusting that the former pastor will not interfere with congregational life nor with the successor's ability to lead, and that any problems which do arise can be resolved amicably.

However, there is often a strong temptation to keep in touch with a former parish and some of its members, which is understandable, considering that the willingness to enter into a deep, committed relationship with a congregation and its people is an essential part of effective pastoring. When that relationship comes to an end, particularly if the relationship has been healthy, a pastor is concerned that the people he or she cared for will continue to be cared for well. It is usually easer for the departed pastor to keep an appropriate distance if the new pastor seems to be doing well. But if cherished ministries that took enormous energy to develop and implement begin to be compromised, if well established traditions and norms are disregarded or trampled, or if pastoral needs go unmet, the temptation for the departed pastor to raise questions, give advice, offer criticism, commiserate about how much better things used to be, or otherwise meddle may grow irresistible.

Yet these temptations must be resisted. For the problems arising in a former parish are the responsibility, first of all, of that parish and its pastor, and then of governing bodies and denominational officials, not of the former pastor. No pastor wants a predecessor second-guessing or interfering with his or her work; likewise, a former pastor must avoid intervention, no matter how well-meant. Meddling is often the spoiled fruit of an egotism that believes, "What I did and how I did it must be preserved!"

Does that mean there can be no contact whatsoever between a pastor and the people of a former congregation? No. But it does mean that such contact needs to be above board and well considered.

A telephone conversation with one's successor is a good context in which to set forth how one intends to behave towards the former congregation and its members. One guideline is to assure the new pastor that you will not agree to any requests from parishioners to baptize, visit, marry, or bury. In fact, a commitment to say simply, "I'm sorry, but I cannot do that, much as it means to me to be invited to do so" is important to make, both for the new pastor and the old. Why? Because these contacts and occasions deepen the relationship between a pastor and his or her congregation. To take them away from the new pastor is to undermine the developing relationship between the congregation and him or her. Again, no one wants this sort of interference in their ministry.

To press the point further, it is even inappropriate to say to the requesting parishioner, "I'd really like to, but your new pastor will have to make the request." Responding like this leaves the new pastor only the possibility of appearing petty and selfish by not issuing such an invitation. There may an occasion when the new pastor does indeed want to involve the old, particularly if a traumatic death comes early in his new ministry, but the initiative must lie always, and freely, with the new pastor.

Another component of this phone call can be a listing of those congregants the departed pastor counts as personal friends, with whom he or she hopes to remain in contact socially. The emphasis here is on "socially." Again, assurance should be given that if and when one is with old friends, one will not talk church gossip or politics. If the friendships are genuine, there will be plenty of topics for conversation other than what is, or is not, going on at church under the new pastor's leadership. And since no one else will be monitoring it, the former pastor must keep to this commitment.

But what if word reaches one's ears that all is not well in a former parish? Such things do happen, and when they do, it is only natural to feel concern. In such cases, one's best recourse is to pray for the congregation and its new pastor, and keep out of the situation, trusting that the good people with whom one worked and helped to grow in faith will do what is best for the congregation.

What the former pastor can and should do in this phone call, however, is to offer to be of service to his or her successor in any way the new pastor feels is necessary. Some new pastors will want to explore the parish and its life all on their own; others will want to pick the former pastor's brain for help in understanding a context that is new to them. Here again, the successor sets the agenda.

Pastor Beth moved to a new congregation about two hundred miles from her former church, where she had enjoyed a remarkably happy and fruitful twelve years of ministry. At her farewell dinner, her ministry had been described as "one long love feast that overflowed into many lives." Beth had decided to leave primarily because she felt everyone, herself included, was becoming too comfortable with the status quo. Her challenges to the congregation to think and find and live in new dimensions of faithfulness were received without resistance or irritation, but not responded to with much energy. Congregational life — in worship, education, fellowship, and mission — was strong but "blissfully stagnating," as Beth described it to her clergy support group about eighteen months before she moved.

Beth's successor was dramatically different. He was an artist, and his vision for the church involved integrating the arts at many points of the congregation's ministry. Within months of his arrival, there was a new coffee house ministry, a gallery for local artists' displays, and a drama group (in which the new pastor participated) that regularly led worship. Beth made a contact phone call like the one described above and enjoyed her conversation with the new pastor, who asked a number of insightful and creative questions.

But after a little while, former parishioners started calling, allegedly "just to chat" or to inquire how Beth liked her new church or to see if she might be coming back for a visit or if she knew about someone's illness. Beth could sense undercurrents of discontent. It wasn't so much that people resented the changes the new pastor was making; in fact, most found the innovations interesting and exciting. But Beth guessed that her successor might not have pastoral care quite as close to the top of his ministerial priority list as she did. Nevertheless, she firmly resisted the temptation to share this suspicion with anyone. Rather, when called, she talked about her new ministry, gently but firmly led the conversation away from talking about her former parish, and brought the call to a close as quickly as possible. In short, she didn't take the bait. The calls soon diminished in frequency, and Beth continued to hold her old congregation in her prayers.

There is, of course, another reason to strictly limit contact with one's former congregation. Looking back longingly will inevitably draw attention and energy away from the new work at hand. The pastor who has gone on to serve a new congregation but who is routinely juggling requests for service from former parishioners or providing a sympathetic ear to those disgruntled over what the new pastor is or is not doing cannot possibly be fully present to the new congregation to which he has been called (and which, incidentally, is compensating him!). Thus, the negative consequences of not being truly gone when one has left accrue to both the former and present congregation. In the end, the only thing served is the pastoral ego.

If the pastoral transition is to retirement, other issues may present themselves. In recent years it has become somewhat more common for pastors to retire in or near the communities of their last pastorate. In such circumstances, there is considerable potential for interference in their former parish's life, even unintentionally. A retired-in-the-community pastor will need to exhibit uncommon discipline so as not to become a problem to his or her successor. Indeed, one appropriate rule of thumb is to not even darken the church door for a full year after one's leave-taking.

But there can be positive outcomes in such circumstances as well. There have been many cases in which the retired pastor has been succeeded by a considerably younger pastor who is secure enough to ask the retiree, as well as his or her spouse, to continue to be part of the congregation and in some cases to serve as a mentor. In such cases, the congregation does not feel that the beloved, now retired, pastor has been cast out and forced to find another church for worship and fellowship — a perception that can cause subconscious resentment toward the newcomer. And the retired pastor may come to have a well-defined, but limited, role. This role might involve occasionally filling in at the pulpit in the new pastor's absence, supporting the congregation's educational ministry by teaching or leading Bible study, helping out with non-member weddings or funerals, or perhaps doing some routine pastoral visitation. Sometimes such a relationship is formalized through the governing board or the denomination with a clear specification of responsibilities. Whether made into a formal arrangement or not, the success of such a situation is absolutely dependent on the retiree's commitment to support the new pastor in every way possible.

Pastor Mark retired and bought a home in the community where he had served his last congregation. He and his wife enjoyed the climate, had a number of fast friends in the community, and were not too far from their children and grandchildren. Mark had informed his denominational officials of his desire and intention to remain in the community, and they had, in turn, cautioned him about his relationship with his former congregation. The week following his last Sunday, even before they had fully unpacked all their belongings in their new house, Mark and his wife left for a three-month trip in their motor home so as to give his newly appointed successor (a second-career minister in his mid-thirties) time and space to get settled in.

A week after Mark and his wife returned, Mark's successor paid them a call. They hit it off immediately. Mark felt the younger man's energy and ideas were just what the congregation needed and was pleased to find that they agreed theologically. Mark shared how glad he was to be free from committee work, how he expected to be doing some guest preaching here and there, and how he was eager to get back to his woodworking once he and his wife were more settled into their new home.

For his part, Mark's successor had previously spoken with denominational higher-ups, who had uniformly described Mark as gracious, centered, and compassionate. One individual had said, "If there's any pastor who won't make problems for you, it's Mark." And so, at the end of the visit, Mark was invited to worship with his former church whenever he wished. This call turned out to be the first of several visits by the new pastor, and a friendship soon blossomed between Mark and his successor. Mark felt his advice, when requested, was appreciated. Over time, he was asked to preach on occasion and to do some pastoral calling. He also did the occasional funeral, mostly for community folks who were not members of his former church. After about a year, Mark asked that his responsibilities be clearly delineated by the church board, and this request was honored. And his successor was blessed to have found both a mentor and a wise, supportive friend in his own congregation.

IN GENERAL, after an initial supportive contact with one's successor, maintaining distance from the former congregation, both physically and emotionally, is a wise and prudent choice for a departed pastor. This frees the former congregation to enter into the work of developing a good relationship with its new pastor, and it frees the former pastor to develop such a relationship with his or her new congregation. While it may not always be true that "good fences make good neighbors," to quote Robert Frost's famous poem, there are times when this is most assuredly so. Setting appropriate behavioral boundaries with a former congregation is crucial for the well-being of everyone involved. There may very well be times when a former pastor is invited back — an anniversary celebration or building dedication, for example. If appropriate boundaries have been observed, these will be occasions of even greater joy, as when two old friends greet each other after a long separation.

· X ·

Thou Shalt Grieve

"Grieve, but not as those who have no hope."

I THESSALONIANS 4:13B

You have done all your farewells. You have left good feelings and good summaries behind. You have done what you can to resolve conflict and reconcile relationships. You have looked to the needs of your self, your friends, and your family. You have stayed away once you have left. There is only one more task necessary in order to leave well.

You must grieve.

Perhaps it feels like this is exactly what you have been doing all through the process of leaving. And truly, many of the actions laid out in these commandments will help with the essential parts of grief work. But some grieving can only be done once the separation is completed, the move is made, and the former context is gone.

Grieving does not come easily in our culture. After a loss of any kind — the death of a loved one, a miscarriage, the loss of a job, an empty nest — the message people often receive, even from well-meaning church members, is,

"Aren't you over that yet?" This response is so deeply in-grained that we sometimes even ask the question of our-selves! But the Bible teaches something different: that the appropriate response to a loss is grief.

After the tragic and horrifying events of September 11, 2001, well-intentioned national leaders urged citizens to "get back to normal" as quickly as possible, to go shopping, to go to sporting events, to take vacations. On the whole, the message seemed to be, "Don't grieve. Don't take all the time necessary to deal with the deep, life-altering losses that have befallen us all." Surely a new way of seeing our nation's role in the world was needed, but this could only be found if we first grieved: grieved not only the loss of so many lives, but also our il-lusion that the great oceans to our east and west some-how insulate us from the rest of the world. The denial of loss only buries the hurt, and such responses are utterly inappropriate for Christians who know the path to new life must always lead to the cross and through the tomb. We do not worship a God who is a cheerleader on the sidelines of life, urging us to get over our losses as quickly as possible. We worship a God who accompanies us through life's valleys and through those days shad-owed by loss.

And yet once we are in retirement or serving with a new congregation, there is an understandably strong temptation to throw ourselves — heart, mind, body, and soul — into the new challenges. So much to learn, so many people to get to know, so many new possibilities! Who has time to grieve? The wise pastor, that's who. The one who knows a pastoral transition is not finished at the completion of a physical move. The one who knows there are feelings yet to experience, longings to talk over with loved ones, and perhaps a letter to be written.

As Pastor Angela settled in with her new congregation, she was pleased that her impressions of the church had been accurate and that many of her hopes for a new pastorate promised to be realized. She liked the people and sensed that some of them would become fast friends. The house she and her husband had bought had a big yard with room for the gardens she had longed to create. The congregation regularly expressed that they were delighted with her leading of worship, especially her preaching. She felt immensely grateful for her new position.

But she still woke up in the morning worrying about what else she might have done at her previous church. She missed her friends; phone calls, e-mails, and cards were a comfort, but just did not provide the same sense of connection. She had heard about old programs being altered, and new programs being put in place. She wondered if a certain couple would stick with much-needed counseling work to save their marriage. She agonized about a closeted gay man who had confided in her. Some of the aged and sick had died, and she missed the privilege of officiating at their funerals. The plain fact of never again seeing so many people she had cared for gnawed at her. Even though she had said her goodbyes well, she found lingering ties that bound her to the church she had loved serving for nine years.

Eventually, Angela mentioned these things to her husband, who responded that he wondered why she had been sleeping so poorly, given how hard she was working. They decided to take time once a week to sit down and share all they were missing — the people, places, and activities that had shaped their previous life. They did this after dinner, with a cup of coffee and a candle burning before them. These conversations brought healing and relief through some tears, some laughter, some deep sighs, some long silences. And week by week they worked through some of the hurt and sense of loss until after a while the once-a-week sharing time began to happen every two weeks, then every three. And by the end of six months, they happened only as needed.

For those pastors who are parents, this kind of intentional sharing should certainly involve the children. Parents can help their children (and each other) by encouraging them to talk about their losses with as much detail as possible, so that larger, global feelings of loss can be gently moved to particular people, places, and activities. And the children should be allowed to adjust to the new location at their own pace. Appreciation of the new context will come in time, and be solidly held, if it is not forced or hurried.

Pastor Gene took a different approach. As part of his spiritual discipline, he wrote in his journal each morning and used many pages in the early days of his new pastorate to name what he was missing from his previous parish. This simple act drained away some of the strongest feelings and allowed him to engage his new work more fully. It also led him to write two letters to his former congregation. The first was overflowing with all the longings he had for his previous, beloved congregation. He went into great detail about individual members (and their quirks) that he missed and the small routines of his life that he missed as well: walking his dog by the river late at night to wind down after a meeting, stopping at a local coffee shop on his way to the office each morning. This letter he wisely chose never to send, recognizing that it had helped him more to write it than it would his old congregation to read it.

Gene's second letter was much more considered. In it, he still shared a few of the things he missed most, but spent most of his words reiterating his gratitude for having had the privilege of serving the congregation, naming what he had learned while with them, and sharing some of the new possibilities that were before him at his new church. He closed with a benediction asking God's blessing on the congregation and its journey with its new pastor. He sent this letter to the pastor, requesting that it be printed in the church newsletter.

After writing these two letters, Gene also decided it would be wise to share some of his grieving with his new congregation. The church had a weekly newsletter, and Gene wrote a few short articles in it about his journey through grief. He shared how his faith spoke to each of the various aspects commonly experienced in response to any significant loss — disorientation, sadness, questioning, and restructuring. So that his new congregation would know that he also felt joy to be with them, Gene was careful to make sure he balanced these articles with others focused on discoveries and hopes and dreams for what lay ahead.

Gene was surprised by how strongly and favorably his new congregation reacted to his grief articles. He came to realize how many people had become conditioned either to hide their grief or to avoid it altogether. His honest sharing had clearly helped others understand the importance of grieving as an essential Christian activity. Eventually, he started a bereavement group for those experiencing any kind of loss. The group thrived, and eventually it took on a life of its own without needing Gene's continuing leadership. Gene's attentiveness to his own grief became a model of Christian grieving, and through it he learned just how important this aspect of ministry can be when so much of life is touched by grief, especially as we grow older.

Both Angela and Gene found ways to ritualize their grief — an essential task for dealing with the lingering emotional ties to a former church. Certainly pastors, who officiate at the rituals that mark the crucial turning points of life — baptism, confirmation, marriage, death — should know the importance of rituals for effective transitions. It is not only permissible but necessary to ritualize our own grief as well, even if the ritual is something small and private — some pastors, for example, hang a picture or two of previous churches in their office as a reminder to themselves of where they have been and to those who come by that the pastor has also had deep ties with other of God's people in other places.

Perhaps we would like to believe that endings and beginnings are clearly demarcated: "That was then, and this is now, and never the twain shall meet." But if we have worked with the dying in our pastoral ministry, we know better. In the dying process, there often comes a kind of bridging between this world and the next. Even while the dying person is still interacting with others around him, he may also be seeing or dreaming of loved ones who have preceded him in death, as if he has a foot in both worlds. Likewise, after we have lost a loved one, we often find ourselves still speaking to her or anticipating her phone call or thinking of the next time we are together. These are all expected, natural parts of loss and grief.

It is no different in making a pastoral transition. Before we have concluded our service with the old congregation, our thoughts are turning to what the new congregation will be like. After we have arrived at the new field of service, we miss the old congregation like the old, worn bathrobe we never wanted to part with. Beginnings and endings are never clear-cut, and grief helps us recognize this.

ACCEPTING THAT GRIEF is a necessary part of pastoral change is a needed last step for successfully leaving a congregation. Take the necessary time to feel and respond to all that wells up within so that you can begin the task of creating new and rich memories in a new setting. "Blessed are those who mourn, for they shall be comforted," said Jesus (Matthew 5:4). And, as always, he knew whereof he spoke. No mourning, no comfort. And no freedom to give ourselves wholly to the new.

The Eleventh Commandment

"Jesus set his face to go to Jerusalem."

LUKE 9:51

The gift born of a faithful departing is the freedom to embrace the new, whether that be retirement, a new pastorate, or a vocation other than ministry. However, too often we live according to what is sometimes called "The First (and Only) Law of Wingwalking." Wingwalking was a daredevil practice in the early days of aviation in which aviators walked the wings of biplanes as they buzzed over airfields, and the first law of wingwalking is this: never let go of what you are holding on to until you are holding on to something else. It is a more than prudent approach to daredevil stunts, but as a strategy for the life of faith in general, and for making a pastoral move in particular, it is less than helpful.

To be fit and free for a new call (or for retirement), we need to prayerfully release our grip on what has gone before, whether it has been a blessing or a curse. Relinquishing the past may be easier when it has been unpleasant or less than satisfying, but it always requires intentionality. We are not free to receive if our hands are tightly clinging to what has been, but only if we open ourselves to the newness that awaits in the future. This releasing, this handing over, is done as a continuing act of prayer in the months of parting and on into the beginning of the new work. The concrete steps set forth in these ten commandments need to be taken within the context of our supplications that God will help us to release our often too-tight grip on what has been.

There came a moment in Jesus' ministry when he set his face toward Jerusalem: he chose to take that next, crucial step. Such moments come to every pastor, and the freedom to set our hearts toward a new call with a new congregation is a great blessing. Releasing that which formerly claimed so much of our energy and devotion is essential to receiving this freedom. Loose ends, late night thoughts of "I wish I had . . . ," regrets over words spoken or not spoken, guilt over not having left behind as great a measure of clarity as possible — all these things can follow and plague the pastor making a vocational transition. We cannot give ourselves wholly to the new work while always casting glances back to our previous ministry.

In spite of how we sometimes speak, we know in our heart of hearts that no congregation is "ours." Congregations are not possessions, but partnerships between a pastor and a people. At most, pastors are the stewards of their congregations, those who have been entrusted with their care, well-being, and development. Remembering this important truth will allow us, in faith, to release a congregation with our blessing into other hands so that our own hands might be free and open for a new experience of faithfulness in which our spiritual growth will unfold. It is not always easy to trust that the work we began with a congregation will be continued and expanded upon by others, but trust we must.

It is sometimes said that the inability to change the past is the one limitation that God shares with us. The best we can do when it comes to leaving a congregation is to bring the past to as complete and whole a conclusion as possible, so that all may rejoice in what has been good, learn from what has not, and move freely and faithfully forward into a promising future where God may be praised and served.